_____
Property of

_____
Address

_____
City/Town

_____
State

From month and year _____ *To month and year* _____

THE
BACKYARD BIRDER'S
JOURNAL

by Howard Blume

SIERRA CLUB BOOKS · *San Francisco*

The Sierra Club, founded in 1892 by John Muir, has devoted itself to the study and protection of the earth's scenic and ecological resources—mountains, wetlands, woodlands, wild shores and rivers, deserts and plains. The publishing program of the Sierra Club offers books to the public as a nonprofit educational service in the hope that they may enlarge the public's understanding of the Club's basic concerns. The point of view expressed in each book, however, does not necessarily represent that of the Club. The Sierra Club has some sixty chapters coast to coast, in Canada, Hawaii, and Alaska. For information about how you may participate in its programs to preserve wilderness and the quality of life, please address inquiries to Sierra Club, 730 Polk Street, San Francisco, CA 94109.

Library of Congress Cataloging-in-Publication Data

Blume, Howard, 1936–
   The backyard birder's journal.

  Bibliography: p.
  1. Bird watching.   I. Title.
QL677.5.B53 1987   598'.07'234   86–3873
ISBN 0-87156-767-9

Production Manager: Susan Ristow

Cover design by Howard Blume

Book design by Bonnie Smetts

Printed in the United States of America

10 9 8 7 6 5 4 3 2 1

Dedicated to Archaeopteryx, Amy Baldwin, and my daughter Robin

CONTENTS

PREFACE

THIS JOURNAL provides a format for keeping a permanent record of all the birds that nest on, pass through, or reside at the habitat you call home; this record is known as the Backyard List.

The journal's pages are organized by season and by the month. It is possible to record, under each month, several consecutive years of lists and observations; this gives you the opportunity to compare, at a glance, the arrival and departure dates, species seen, and any notes and observations of previous years with your most recent entry. There are special sections designed for you to record your Backyard Life List, Backyard Big Year, Backyard Big Day, Backyard Nesting Birds, Backyard Christmas Count, and Backyard Rarities.

Until now there were no existing formats that satisfied the needs of the Backyard List. Other lists birders keep are usually filed away.

Because your backyard birds are always available when you are available—which is whenever you are at home—your *Backyard Birder's Journal* should be kept out, accessible for immediate entry or reference.

The Backyard Birder's Journal is intended for all levels of birders, but you don't have to be a birder to keep the journal. Living with your backyard is all that is necessary; your backyard birds will do the rest—they'll provide the incentives.

Since the Backyard List centers around the home and can often involve several members of a family, it can operate on several different levels; it can be a record, not only of the changes and events of the avifauna in your backyard, but also of the changes and events of your family and home. Thus, I believe, it is a list with a heart.

ACKNOWLEDGMENTS

NOT EVERY literary agent would have bothered to submit *The Backyard Birder's Journal*. Ellen Levine did. She believed in it, and she isn't a birder.

Not every editor would select *The Backyard Birder's Journal* out of a pile of manuscripts all asking to be published. Diana Landau, a senior editor for Sierra Club Books, discovered the book. She believed in it, and she isn't a birder.

Before Diana and I could get together and go over the manuscript she left Sierra Club Books. Sometimes enthusiasm for a project wanes during the transition of editors. So when James Cohee, my new senior editor, took over the project I was apprehensive—until I talked to him on the phone. He bowled me over with his enthusiasm and continued to do so throughout the project. Jim's encouragement and guidance allowed me the opportunity to explore, clarify, and ultimately make my own decisions and find my own voice.

Jim also appointed Mary Anne Stewart as my copy editor, which was another way he took good care of me. Throughout the work, Mary Anne kept me clear, organized, and honest, and when needed, she provided insight and inspiration. That she happens to be a birder was an added bonus for me and the journal.

Thank you all.

I would also like to thank Roger Tory Peterson for taking time out of his busy schedule to gather, tabulate, and key his Backyard Life List. Thanks also go to Almena Gudas, Merlin Killpack, Dan Murphy, and Harvey Williams for enthusiastically contributing their backyard lists and experiences. And a thank you to all the other birders who eagerly responded to my backyard queries.

THE
BACKYARD BIRDER

INTRODUCTION

I BELIEVE most of us possess the soul, if not the passion, of a birder, and that doesn't presuppose taking to the field to watch birds. What it implies is your innate capacity to enjoy and appreciate the avifauna; if someone called your attention to a wild bird carrying out its natural history, you would experience some pleasure, wonder, and maybe a rush of excitement followed by a smile. Then you would go about your business—but not without being transformed in some small but crucial way.

What we can get from birds is a lifetime of accumulated pleasures. After spending several years noticing birds, you'll find yourself deriving from a fleeting encounter, a far-off silhouette, or a burst of song a sense of knowing and, subsequently, a feeling of satisfaction and well-being; even the briefest contact with a particular species of bird will conjure up all the other times, all the other past events associated with that bird. For instance, hurrying through my backyard on my way to the car I hear, or see in the periphery of my vision, for an instant, a White-breasted Nuthatch. This brief episode conjures up a condensation of winters spent looking out the window watching White-breasted Nuthatches at our feeder: watching their distinct swoop in to approach the feeder; watching their mechanical swift meanderings up and down a tree; watching them hang upside down while jamming a sunflower seed into a crevice of bark and then beat-ing the seed open with their bills; watching their black, gray, and white design boldly drawn along their sleek, powerful bodies. Essence of White-breasted Nuthatch stored in a microstack of human neurons. Something inside is touched and released, and a millisecond of pleasure pulses through me; I go through a metaphysical self-satisfied smirk, and I'm not fully aware of it until I am sitting on the commuter train staring out the window. And if I continue to stare out the window and happen to see the distant silhouettes of cormorants strung out single file, flying low over the Hudson River, the process begins all over again.

These episodes can happen anytime and anywhere. Anywhere.

A breeze blew in from Lake Michigan, skirting off the steel, glass, stone, and marble skyscrapers onto the crowds below. It was a beautiful, exuberant, brilliant, sunny May day in the city of Chicago. My partner and I talked business strategies, soaked up the day, and walked among crowds of fellow cosmopolitans on their noon-hour lunch break.

The episode was in progress as we crossed the street, at the intersection of Wacker and Michigan Avenue, where the Michigan Avenue Bridge spans the Illinois River. Reaching the bridge, we came to the back of a small crowd, their attention focused on the pavement. Both of us squeezed through, expecting to see a street performer or a human tragedy. Instead we saw an exhausted Wood Thrush, propped up on the glaring pavement, its wings drooping, its feathers puffed out, its mouth agape, and its breathing deep and labored. If it were a pigeon grounded on the pavement there would be no commotion; but this noon-hour crowd knew that this bird, about the size of a robin, with a brown back, rust-orange head, and dark spots on its chest, didn't belong in the city. Suddenly a teenage boy grabbed the bird and headed for the edge of the bridge. He was about to fling the bird into the river. I grabbed the Wood Thrush from his hand, told my partner I'd see him later, and hailed a cab.

The Wood Thrush was on its way to its northern nesting grounds. It began its migration possibly from southern Texas, Mexico, or maybe even Panama. While flying over the city of Chicago, looking for a place to land and replenish, the thrush ran out of steam. I sat in the back seat of the cab, holding the bird in my hands, hands resting in my lap. Now its breathing was normal and its mouth closed; it was calm and didn't struggle. I've held thrushes before, and they do struggle. The dim light and quiet in the back seat of a Yellow Cab proved to be a better place for a Wood Thrush than Michigan Avenue at noon. I told the cabby that this could very well be the first Wood Thrush that spent part of its migration north in a Yellow Cab. The cabby was pleased to be part of the migration. So was I.

We stopped at the Lincoln Park Sanctuary, a remnant of woods and marsh enclosed by a cyclone fence. (The sanctuary is a minute fraction of the Chicago park system along Lake Michigan.) I stepped up to the cyclone fence and carefully placed the bird's head in an opening facing the woods. I didn't even get a chance to open my hands. The trees thirty feet off were what that Wood Thrush needed to see. All I did was loosen my grip, and it slipped away, like water between my fingers; two seconds later it was lost in the woods.

Encountering birds in the heart of the city, especially migratory birds, isn't that uncommon. I've knelt on my knees in a city parking lot, my face a foot away from the opened bills and pink mouths of three exhausted Ruby-crowned Kinglets perched side by side on the branch of a four-foot skinny tree of heaven growing out of a crack in the asphalt. If I were a cat I could have swallowed the kinglets. I did swallow them, with my eyes and heart. They weighed two grams, were three to four inches long, and as tough as they were cute. Crowds buzzed by us. Cars squeezed in and out of the lot. Life went on. As soon as the birds recovered, they'd scour the leaves for insects and then fly off, continuing their migration to Canada, where they'd find themselves a spruce tree to nest in. Every spring I've spent in Chicago, I've seen kinglets, temporarily tucked in among the skyscrapers. Given this kind of avian activity in the bare city, one can imagine what goes on in an urban or suburban backyard with so much more to offer.

Backyards provide us with all kinds of possibilities. Besides spring and fall migratory birds, backyards have their resident birds, their nesting birds, their wintering birds, and their surprises—the unexpected bird. Every season brings to your backyard its complement of birds, and every day in your backyard, birds play out their natural histories.

If you have a backyard, even if it is a small one, you will eventually be touched by your backyard birds; it's inevitable. Birds are your most accessible entry into the natural world. Birds are pervasive. Even if you are cooped up inside your home, you still will be able to hear and see them from a window.

My brother Phillip and his wife, Jinny, began to feed their backyard birds in Lincolnwood, Illinois, in the winter, sharing the experience with their three young children. Soon they bought a field guide and binoculars. Now they feed their birds year round, and Phillip brags about the birds he gets at the feeder. He told me how in one sitting he saw around his feeder a Red-headed Woodpecker, an Indigo Bunting, an American Goldfinch, and a Northern Cardinal. He was overwhelmed by that collective display of color. Phillip is hooked. And he's not a birder nor ever will be.

Colette and Lowell are two writer friends whose backyard is 125 feet above a mountain river in Woodstock, New York. Innocently enough, they set out their first feeder, not knowing what to expect from the birds or themselves. After several days the birds responded, and so did Colette and Lowell.

Within a short time their backyard birds were incorporated into their daily routine, giving them a whole new way of living with their backyard and a new lease on life. Their morning cup of coffee and their afternoon break would never be the same. Chickadees, titmouses, woodpeckers, and nuthatches were there for them on a daily basis. Every once in a while a strange new bird would materialize, throwing them into a state. Colette was held spellbound one day when she looked up from her typewriter out her studio window and saw a combination of feathers, form, and color she'd never seen before, perched four feet away in a tree above the river. She ran to her field guide and identified the bird as a Belted Kingfisher. Colette and Lowell were pleased to find the kingfisher was nesting along the bank below their backyard, giving them the opportunity to see this striking-looking bird and hear its rattle-shriek throughout the summer and on into the fall. After a year and a half, Lowell felt that they'd seen enough birds in their backyard to warrant keeping a list.

Colette and Lowell began a Backyard List, and they're a long way off from being called birders. But they, like my brother, have the soul of a birder. Most people do. Your backyard is the place to make that discovery. Your backyard journal is the place to record it.

In gathering material and data for this journal I corresponded with birders from all over the country and found that the Backyard List was diligently kept and enjoyed by most. To most hard-core birders the Backyard List doesn't carry the same weight as some of the other lists they keep, but it's a list kept just the same; there isn't one birder worth his binoculars who can be in his backyard and ignore a migratory wave in progress, a bird at the feeder, or the opportunity to add a new bird to the list. The pressure is off in the backyard. You can sit back with your beer or cup of herb tea and let birds come as they may; and they will, that's a guarantee.

Keeping in touch with his backyard birds and keeping a Backyard List and journal provide a birder with a record of seasonal expectations to look forward to and keeps him alert for the unexpected. The Backyard List also offers a birder a modicum of competition and much self-satisfaction. Ludlow Griscon, the patron saint of American birding, has a Backyard Life List of 180 species seen from his home in Cambridge, Massachusetts. That's an impressive number for a Backyard Life List, and a hard one to approach, yet alone beat (unless you live in California, where Backyard Life Lists have comfortably topped the 210 mark). I am sure that Ludlow Griscon's many outstanding accomplishments in ornithology did not preempt the pleasure and satisfaction he got from pursuing and keeping his Backyard List; the list reflects his skill as a birder and his love for birds and birding. Larry Balch, president of the American Birding Association and one of the top birders in the country, has a Backyard Life List of 95 species seen from his home in Lincolnwood, Illinois. He doesn't work at it, but if he did, Larry says he'd have a Backyard Life List of 150. That was said with the complete confidence of a birder who intimately knows his birds and the potential of his backyard. No bird will go unidentified if he hears or sees it, even if it be for the briefest moment. When asked what backyard sightings were of note, Larry mentioned, with a measured amount of pride, a Clay-colored Sparrow, Mourning Warbler, and two individual sightings of a Northern Shrike, each seen on two bitter-cold midwest Januaries. I was impressed.

Throughout the years I have come to the conclusion that the Backyard List is as important as any of the other lists birders keep and covet, maybe even more so. Since most of us spend a consistent amount of time at our homes, we have the opportunity to accumulate thorough life histories and records of our backyard birds. If kept carefully throughout the years, these could prove to be invaluable data.

Suburbia has affected avian populations; some species have taken to the suburbs, some haven't. The backyard journal is a record of avian density and variety in your backyard; a record of what species have taken to your backyard and how. You, the keeper of the journal, become the keeper of the flock, becoming sensitive to the changes and fluctuations of your backyard birds. If a resident species disappears or a nesting species doesn't turn up one season, you will be there to record and experience the loss. If a new species takes up residence or passes through, you'll be the first to record and celebrate its arrival.

No one has of yet, as far as I know, thoroughly compiled the backyard data from throughout the country and fed it into a computer. Suburbia, even though it offers a modicum of habitats, covers a great deal of territory; it deserves the attention. If a representative sampling of backyard lists were collected from all over the country, then published and made available on a yearly basis, it would supplement the existing surveys, providing a broader and more comprehensive picture of avian populations.

Your backyard journal in time will accrue a certain market value. When our home was up for sale I found it difficult to exclude my Backyard List from the enticing extras homeowners include with the description of the house. My journal was offered for perusal to all prospective buyers. After all, a Backyard Life List of 103 species isn't a number to sneeze at. And who can boast 3 species of nesting thrushes forty minutes from Manhattan.

That's not such a bad idea; xerox your Backyard Life List and some of your other pertinent backyard records and give them to your lawyer to present along with the deed to the owners-to-be. The responsibility and pleasure of keeping a record of backyard birds could be transferred from the old owner to the new owner, as we transfer, as a matter of course and without discussion, the appreciation and care of all the flowers and shrubs we have planted, nurtured, and enjoyed over the years. This would make a fine tradition and provide a long-term continuing surveillance of avian populations and the backyards they depend on.

BIRDERS AS LISTERS

THERE ISN'T another class of vertebrates that has inspired the human race to make lists the way the Class Aves has. Birding seems to be synonymous with list keeping.

Why Birders Keep Lists

A novice birder usually begins his first list in self-defense against the initial onslaught of new birds: it's the only way to keep track. But there's a lot more to list keeping than keeping track.

Those very first lists, kept during your first few days out birding, and kept probably on a scrap of whatever paper is available, have an insidious habit of leading you on a step further. A day's birding can give a novice birder the pleasure of the immediate experience but leave very little visual memory of birds seen. The list takes you to your field guide, where you can sustain the pleasure, and where the obscure little Warbling Vireo seen singing and feeding high up in the branches of an oak tree can be reviewed close up, the field marks accentuated, etched into your mind for the next time out.

The field guide, in turn, leads to more list keeping. Roger Tory Peterson's *Field Guide to the Birds* deserves a good portion of the blame for turning me into a list keeper. I believe most birders weaned on Peterson or some other well-rendered field guide have gone through a similar metamorphosis. Once I thumbed through page after page of appetizingly rendered birds, neatly displayed like colored candied treats in a display case, I was primed. Peterson's pages are full of rich potential, which soon becomes rich expectation.

All it takes is one good spring migration, one good day of birding at a local park, marsh, forest preserve, or your own backyard, to discover that all those rendered birds in the field guide aren't remote, exotic species. Even though they might spend a portion of their life in inaccessible wilderness, they still can be seen passing through or visiting for a time on or near your own stomping grounds.

The list soon becomes a realization of expectations, tangible evidence of your career as a birder. You become a collector—like a stamp, coin, or butterfly collector—except that you collect the names of birds, and in each name is the verification of a species' existence and your ability to identify it.

The list also provides pleasure and satisfaction on another level that is not so obvious or immediate. Besides being a record of birds seen, the list is a record of your experience, coded in the name of a bird, recalling places, events, and friends. The list becomes a reflection of your life. It is there for you to refer to, connecting the past with the present, bringing to mind a special day, like the spring day when you and two friends standing at the edge of a marsh saw the first White-faced Ibis ever recorded in Illinois. Like the day when, from your kitchen window, you, your wife, and kids saw a Bald Eagle preening its feathers as it perched on a thick limb of your old maple tree. The list becomes an affirmation of your experience to savor in days and years to come.

Whenever I think of birds and bird lists in this context, I think of Amy Baldwin, birder and friend, who passed away several years ago. Before I got to know her personally, I'd see her every once in a while throughout the years, usually trudging through the field with a group of birders half her age; she'd always have a hefty pair of binoculars hanging around her thin, old neck. I met her when she was eighty-six. She rarely went birding then. She spent most of the time alone, in her basement apartment on the south side of Chicago.

The first thing I noticed when I stepped down into Amy's apartment was the baby grand piano that served as the hearth of the room—the place I gravitated toward to warm my hands and talk. On top of the piano was Amy's collection of lifetime mementos—neat stacks of letters and photographs, and among them, stacks of bird lists covering over fifty years of birding. Also resting on the piano was Amy's first and only copy of Peterson's *Field Guide to the Birds*, burnished smooth with a lifetime of use but still in good shape.

Amy pulled a rubber band loose from a packet of pocket-sized black-and-white photographs and showed me a picture of a younger Amy and friend, poised beneath a snow-covered mountain. She had a checklist of birds to go along with that photograph. Amy told me that these days alone in her basement apartment were the happiest days in her life. I found that difficult to believe when held up against the active years of her youth and midlife.

"Creative evaluation" is a term I once found in the *Journal of Creative Behavior* used to describe a life stage that "begins in old age and continues until death; it entails a process of assessment and taking stock of one's life in preparation for one's death. The goal of this period is the acceptance of and satisfaction with one's life." No one had to tell Amy Baldwin about creative evaluation. Those personal collections, those mementos of one's life, are usually stored away from view in suitcases, dresser drawers, and attics. Not so with Amy. She knew what she needed. Those neatly arranged stacks of memories, among them her bird lists, were kept out for touch and review, connecting past with present, providing her with all the activity she needed and allowing her to assess and take stock while basking in the warmth of her life.

A Listing of Lists

First we have, at the head of the list, the Life List—a list of all the birds seen in one's lifetime. One version is the North American Life List, usually kept by all, even the most casual birder. Larry Balch, whose Backyard Life List was discussed earlier, and who is a Chicago math professor and president of the American Birding Association, is far from being a casual birder, with a North American Life List of 760 species. That's 760 out of a possible 826 species of birds that either nest in, pass through, or are accidently whisked into the North American continent. Such a number isn't easy to come by, and it has put Larry in contention for the number-one spot on the list of big listers.

Most birders add to their Life Lists whenever a new bird happens past their binoculars, taking the birds as they come. Serious birders won't take them as they come—they take off in pursuit. The North American Life List becomes a major preoccupation and a competition involving much energy and often much cash. A top goal is to make the 600 Club. To qualify, a birder must identify within the United

States, within one calendar year, a minimum of 600 birds, more than most birders see in a lifetime. Some birders go even further.

Jim Vardaman, president of a forest management firm, spent $44,000 in one year traveling across the country in an attempt to see and list 700 species of birds. He missed his goal by one species. Ken Kaufman, nomad birder, hitchhiked across the country with $1000 in his pocket in pursuit of his Big Year List. He ended up seeing and listing 671 species.

That's enough about the big listers. There isn't much heart in the big list—accomplishment, yes, but not much heart.

Next on the list of lists comes the Big Day List—how many species of birds you can see in one day. You don't have to have the resolution of the big listers to try for a big day. Most birders will give it a go at least once or twice a year, usually during spring or fall migration when birding is best.

Going for a big day usually means traveling by car with a small, intimate group for long as twenty-four hours, driving from predetermined habitat to habitat to get the widest range of species, ducking in and out of cars and moving through the terrain like troops on maneuvers, checking off the birds as soon as identified. It can be a tough, long day, but friends and birds make it all worthwhile. Some groups have used these big-day "birdathons" as spirited fundraisers for environmental causes.

Then there is the Daily List, made every time one goes birding. The data from this simple list can easily be applied to other lists, such as a State List, which in turn can provide one with enough stimulus to go for the state record. It doesn't take much to turn a list into a contest.

Finally we come to the subject of this book, the homely Backyard List—a list of all the birds seen or heard in or from the habitat you call home. A backyard can be anything from the view from your apartment window to the ocean as seen from your home at the beach. The keynote is home: if you can see it from where you live, whether it includes a quarter of an acre or ten, it's your backyard. And, as mentioned in the Introduction, I believe the Backyard List is as important as any of the other lists birders keep and covet, maybe even more so. Since we usually spend a number of years living at one residence along with the same backyard, we can keep a long-term record of our backyard birds; backyard data could one day be part of the overall picture of avian populations. The varieties and how-to's of the Backyard List are taken up later on in *The Backyard Birder's Journal—Putting It to Use*.

Often birders will invent new lists. When I was twelve years old and had just finished a game of softball, I came across a dead Yellow-billed Cuckoo lying near third base. I picked up the bird and held him in my hand for over an hour. I was mesmerized. Even though I wasn't aware of the workings and wonders of random genetic change and natural selection, I knew I was holding an exceptional and exquisite piece of work. It was then I began my Death List, a list I kept for about ten years. It wasn't a large list: there I noted the dead warblers I found beneath the Chicago skyscrapers; the dead loon that fell from the sky, barely missing my head; and all the dead gulls and ducks found on the beach.

A serious-birder friend of mine kept a Dream List, but it never appeared in any of the ornithological journals with the rest of his earthly sightings. I've tried to keep a Dream List, but I could never seem to identify any of the birds.

List Keeping Put to Good Use

Ornithologists may be the only scientists—bio, physical, or otherwise—who can recruit for assistance in their research a work force of amateurs who are there for the asking. Not only are they free of charge, they are usually in place, doing what is required—watching birds and keeping lists. Two of these amateur-assisted research projects are the Christmas Bird Count and the Atlas Project.

The Christmas Bird Count

Picture this scene: winter's cold silence; ten degrees above zero; a procession of six people bundled up in polypropylene, wool, and down feathers crunches through the hard-packed snow, silent, shivering, and alert, each with binoculars. One stops; they all stop, scanning the dark evergreens with their binoculars. One of them calls out, "Two Red Crossbills." When enough members have verified the call, someone opens a small notebook and jots down "2 Red Crossbills." They then tramp off to the frozen edge of a river. They began their day at five in the morning. They'll end it hooting for owls in the dark.

This hardy group is participating in the annual Christmas Count. It takes place any one day during Christmas week all over the country. On the chosen day, small groups of birders scour their own fifteen-mile diameter territories to find and list the winter bird population. For me, the Christmas Count is part of the Christmas celebration—a celebration of life set against a vivid starkness. Every bird becomes a find whose energy is a welcome sign of life, often the only sign of life in the frozen landscape besides the birders, who have come to pay homage, share the day, and keep lists.

I'm not sure I'd have this kind of reverence for the Christmas Count if I lived in Florida, Texas, or California, where the winter bird population isn't as sparse and photosynthesis goes on as usual. It has something to do with celebrating too many Christmases at temperatures at or below thirty-two degrees Fahrenheit. One of these days I'm going to have to ask a Floridian how he feels about his Christmas Count.

Mary Anne Stewart, a Californian who happens to be my copy editor and a birder, upon reading the last paragraph, volunteered her experience of a California Christmas Count:

It's usually cold and wet where my count is out on Point Reyes. You feel like a kid sloshing around in the mud in big rubber boots. You feel a special kinship with the few other people who are crazy enough—or smart enough—to be out in weather like this. And every bird you see is special too, perhaps because there's nobody else to appreciate it but you. And you marvel at how well this fragile little creature is doing in weather that has you bundled up and shivering. Occasionally you curse the bare-branched poison oak you didn't notice as you were moving up on a bird.

The air warms up and you begin to feel pretty smug for doing such a marvelous activity on such a marvelous day, with the sea and green hills sparkling around you. And at nightfall you end up in a rented hall with a hundred other birders, drinking wine and downing a catered dinner while the area compiler runs down the checklist out loud, stopping for exact descriptions of rare bird sightings. And of course, it being California, afterwards you head for a hot tub if you can.

The results of the Christmas Count, all those lists of wintering birds made by all those birders from all over the country, are not filed away among each birder's collection of lists. They are destined for bigger and better use—they are destined to be published. After the count day, the lists are sent to their appropriate regional compiler, who organizes them and sends them off to the Audubon Society headquarters in New York. There the lists are fed into a computer, and eventually every bird, birder, locale, and compiler are accounted for and published in *American Birds*, a magazine serving both professionals and amateurs.

There is something about seeing those lists in print that evokes for me blood, flesh, and feathers. To some, they might read like a dictionary, but to me the lists read like Hemingway. The name of the town and the state, the weather conditions, the temperature, the number of hours spent, the lists of birds seen, the species counted, and the list of participants describe the day so vividly that I am there, and I feel I know not only the birds listed but the birders who reported them—what brand of winter boots each wore and who had cold feet.

The results of the 1983 Christmas Count in Peterborough, Ontario, are reprinted here from the July-August 1984 issue of *American Birds*. Species in boldface type are rare or unusual sightings.

96. **Peterborough, Ont.** 44°20′N 78°22′W, center Chemong Rd. and Sunset Blvd., as described 1972; elevation 625 to 1025 ft; habitat coverage, as described 1979.—Dec. 27; 5:30 A.M. to 5:15 P.M. A.M.: mostly clear. P.M.: mostly cloudy. Temp. 25° to 36° F. Wind light. No snow cover. Water mostly open. Wild food crop good. Nineteen observers, 18 in 13 parties, 1 at feeders. Total party-hours, 99 (56 on foot, 35 by car, 8 by bicycle) plus 4 hours at feeders, 4 owling; total party-miles, 564 (64 on foot, 479 by car, 21 by bicycle) plus 40 miles owling.
• Canada Goose 3; Snow Goose (white form) 5; Mallard 432; Black Duck 3; Mallard X Black Duck 4; **N. Shoveler 1**; Com. Goldeneye 3; Goshawk 2; Sharp-shinned Hawk 1; Cooper's Hawk 1; Red-tailed Hawk 33; Rough-legged Hawk 1; Am. Kestrel 9; Ruffed Grouse 19; **Glaucous Gull 1**; Herring Gull 267; Ring-billed Gull 9; gull, sp. 1; Rock Dove 1291; Mourning Dove 43; Ringed Turtle Dove 1; Great Horned Owl 21; Belted Kingfisher 3; Com. (Yel.-sh.) Flicker 2; Pileated Woodpecker 8; Hairy Woodpecker 49; Downy Woodpecker 66; woodpecker, sp. 2; Blue Jay 235; Com. Crow 126; Black-capped Chickadee 1531; White-breasted Nuthatch 68; Red-breasted Nuthatch 1; Brown Creeper 21; Am. Robin 11; Golden-crowned Kinglet 47; Cedar Waxwing 21; N. Shrike 9; Starling 1586; House Sparrow 1350; Red-winged Blackbird 4; Com. Grackle 1; Brown-headed Cowbird 2; Cardinal 29; Evening Grosbeak 148; Purple Finch 29; Com. Redpoll 2 (low); Pine Siskin 1; Am. Goldfinch 240; Dark-eyed (Slate-col.) Junco 42; Tree Sparrow 474; White-throated Sparrow 2; Swamp Sparrow 5; Song Sparrow 27; Snow Bunting 167.
Total, 51 species (plus 1 hybrid, 1 exotic); 8460 individuals. (In count area count week but not seen count day: Great Blue Heron, **Redhead**, Com. Merganser, **Iceland Gull**.)—Tony Bugg, Rhea Bringeman, Peter Burke, Geoff Carpentier, Jim Cashmore, Alan Green, Fred Helleiner, Peter Hogenbirk, Larry Keeley, *Bill McCord, Ted McDonald, Doug McRae, Al Nicholson, Mike Oldham, Brian Olson, Martin Parker, Ken Rumble, Doug Sadler (compiler—R R 4, Peterborough, Ont. K9J 6X5), David Swales.

The Atlas Project

A breeding-bird atlas is a survey of where in a geographic region each specific species breeds; the breeding data are eventually plotted on a map—thus its name, *atlas*.

A breeding-bird atlas or census is conducted regionally, within the confines of each state; it is sponsored and initiated by scientific organizations, bird clubs, or state environmental departments, which often work in conjunction with each other and recruit birders in the gathering of data.

Here's how the Atlas Project works in the state of New York, which is the way it works in all states: A selected committee divides the state of New York into over five thousand blocks, each block covering three square miles. They then divide the state up into ten regions, appointing a regional coordinator for each. The regional coordinator enlists willing observers, whose skill ranges from novice to veteran birder to professional ornithologist. The regional coordinator gives the observers appropriate guidance and materials and bestows upon them their three-square-mile block. The observers' job for the next five years, every spring and summer, is to find and list all the nesting birds within their block. They are given criteria to follow and make out their lists accordingly.

Breeding evidence falls into three categories:

Possible   A bird is seen in the proper nesting habitat and there are no other signs of breeding, *or*
A male is present and singing, *or*
Breeding calls are heard

Probable   A range of breeding behavior is present, such as birds building a nest or excavating a nest hole

Confirmed   Finding of nest and young

Each species needs to be confirmed only once in each block. The number of birds isn't recorded; observers concentrate on finding new nesting species and upgrading a possible nester to a confirmed nester. The same block can be worked in succeeding years with the aim of confirming all species present.

Real commitment, dedication, and maybe an understanding spouse —that's what it takes to tie five consecutive springs and summers of your life to the same three square miles of territory. The personal benefits are few, but choice. A birder gets the chance to really know the natural history of a place—to become sensitive to its subtle and unique features. He will find himself developing a fondness and yearning for place that will make him feel good every time he recalls his investment in it. Instead of dealing only with a bird's field marks, he will learn to understand and interpret a bird's behavior, to observe and enjoy the nuances. And, as he makes out his lists of probables, possibles, and confirmeds, he might even have the small but distinct satisfaction of discovering a new breeding bird for his state, being the one responsible for putting that bird on the map.

At the end of each nesting season the lists are collected by the regional coordinator and incorporated into a computer data base. Each year's results are added to those of earlier years. The final product will be a regional breeding-bird atlas, a book with distribution maps for each species observed.

Keepers of the Flock

The Christmas Bird Count and endeavors like the Atlas Project provide a base against which to measure future ecological change. These tabulations provide the ornithologist, the legislator, the park commissioner, and the land developer with a kind of avian bookkeeping showing the increases and decreases in bird populations, which species have moved into an area and which have left, and consequently which species and habitats require protection. I find it comforting to know that there are these small but dedicated groups of birders patrolling our earth, watching over the flock, making lists and keeping tabs on the whereabouts and numbers of the avifauna, ready to forecast the first sign of trouble, but there basically to marvel at and enjoy the birds.

FROM BACKYARD LIST TO BACKYARD JOURNAL

IN A MAJOR transition in our life, my wife, kids, and I moved from a city apartment into a house in Irvington, New York, a backwoods suburb in the Hudson River Valley. Our backyard was suddenly four-plus acres, a portion of which was a small woodlot with thick, overgrown patches of brambles. I never thought to ask the previous owner what the birding was like. Was I in for a surprise!

The first spring migration in our backyard gave me a decisive wallop. Morning after morning we woke to commotion: the trees were jam-packed with the singing and buzzings of warblers and songbirds. They were all there, right out of the pages of my well-worn Peterson's *Field Guide*. All those birds I'd scoured the countryside for were now surrounding my house. Even the difficult ones, the ones you have to beat the bushes for, like the Mourning Warbler and White-eyed Vireo, hid out in our brambles.

What great luck, I thought. What great luck, to have selected such a prolific, bird-producing property. But it had nothing to do with luck. What I didn't realize at the time was that every backyard in the United States gets its share of spring migration. All backyards are blessed with the color, singing, and energy of birds, waves of birds inundating tree and shrub, there for those who have the eyes and ears to see and hear them. The miracle of migration is a step outside anyone's front or back door. Once I began to compare backyard notes with other birders throughout the country I realized that we are all lucky.

Then I discovered the nesting birds. First was a Rose-breasted Grosbeak nest. The most I had expected was a robin's. Then I found a Blue-winged Warbler's nest: anyone with a nesting warbler should consider themselves fortunate indeed! There were other nesters as well, but the ultimate gift from our backyard was the nesting thrushes, three species of them—a Wood Thrush, a Veery, and a Swainson's Thrush. They turned our backyard into a cathedral of the divine where chorus after rolling chorus followed our evenings into night. By all rights, to deserve such singing we should be living in the far north woods—not forty minutes by car from Manhattan.

It was unavoidable. There was just too much going on in our backyard. I began to keep a Backyard List.

The Pileated Woodpecker

There has never been a dull season in our backyard. It always has something to offer us in the way of birds; there is always a surprise, always the unexpected.

One early cold, sunny March morning my wife, Kay, and I woke to the loud pounding of a woodpecker, apparently an unusually strong woodpecker beating the dickens out of a tree somewhere out our bedroom window. The two of us took to the window, and there we saw in our backyard the impossible—a Pileated Woodpecker. We were stunned. "Impossible," I said. "What's a Pileated Woodpecker doing in our backyard?" His wings seemed much too large for suburbia. His huge red crest and thick, dagger bill are more at home etched in stone as fossil. He makes much more sense flying over the heads of mastodons than rooftops. The Pileated's livelihood once came from extensive woodlands. Now he's surviving in meager wooded enclaves perforated by highways, shopping centers, and the likes of me. This bird is up to some remarkable adaptation in which all of suburbia is the fortunate beneficiary. My nonbirding neighbors always are eager to exchange Pileated sightings with me.

The appearance of a Pileated Woodpecker in our backyard called for more than just a flat entry of species and date in my Backyard List. I needed space to carry on. The Pileated and other birds often required the form of a journal in which I could record not only their visits but also any observations, concerns, or mullings that might surface following the interaction of man and bird.

So the Backyard List evolved to a backyard journal. The Pileated made it to my backyard journal eight times. The seventh and eighth entries weren't prompted by its sighting but by its absence. "No Pileated this spring," I wrote. "No Pileated this fall. The remnant patches of woodlots gave way to condos. The backyard loses a species."

The Nesting Phoebes and the Nesting Blumes

The Eastern Phoebe is a seven-inch, deep gray brown, tail-bobbing, spunky bird that began its history as a species by building its moss- and lichen-covered nests on the rock shelves of cliffs. Now it has found itself a home in suburbia. Every backyard in eastern America has a nesting phoebe—or if it doesn't, it should have. Life would be so much sweeter.

The phoebe is a regular visitor to our backyard and a regular entry in my backyard journal. Each year on March 26, give or take a few days, a male phoebe arrives at our home. Even though my wife and I await his arrival, he usually catches us off-guard, filtering into our preoccupied consciousness with his emphatic two-note song. Sometime after his song has taken root, one of us will say, "I think the phoebe is back." And the other will reply, "I know. I think I heard him this morning—or was it yesterday morning?"

Then we wait for the female to join him in the eaves of the house where several old nests sit, evidence of past years' labors. Neither one of us can relax and get on with the advent of spring until the female phoebe arrives; to our relief, she always turns up. Then we monitor the phoebes' progress: the repairing of an old nest or the building of a new one, the incubation of eggs, the feeding of young, and the whereabouts of Sam, our cat, whom we find daily sitting beneath the nest waiting for a young bird to drop.

Behavioral biologists call a detailed record of the behavioral patterns of an animal an ethogram. By carefully watching a particular species of bird, one can collect a list of behaviors, such as body care, feeding strategies, social and courtship displays, and so on. Breeding birds such as our phoebes are good subjects for an ethogram because they don't stray far from the nest, making them easy to observe, and they provide a variety of behaviors.

Our involvement with the phoebes found me inadvertently keeping a quasiethogram accompanied by my two cents' worth of commentary. Our interactions were events to make note of; an entry in our backyard journal became the natural history of two families, an ethogram not only of the nesting phoebes but also of the nesting Blumes.

March 18, 1976. Hallelujah, the phoebes are back. Spring is here.

June 24, 1978. Every time Sam would sit or walk beneath their nest, the bird not attending the nest would sound its alarm call as it watched Sam from the perch above. The longer Sam remained, the louder and more rapid the phoebe would chirp. After a while Kay and I reacted as if the alarm notes were directed not only to mate and fledglings but deliberately to us. Maybe they were. Maybe the phoebes eventually caught on and knew that every time one of them would sound its alarm call, Kay or I would run out of the house, grab the cat, and whisk it away. As soon as one of us carried off Sam everything quieted down, and the only sound we would hear from the phoebes was the occasional sharp pop of an insect caught in their bills. It resembles the sound of a snapping finger, but much louder and crisper, like a little explosion. Maybe the sound effect has something to do with the chitenous exoskeleton of the insect. Or the percussion of the bird's bill. Or both. Whatever it is, when we hear it, we know Sam is in the house and all is well with the phoebes.

March 20, 1981. The male phoebe arrived today. He's quiet and aloof, keeping his distance. He won't have to deal with Sam this year. We had to put him to sleep this winter.

Most of the time the Blumes go about their business and the phoebes go about theirs; but there isn't a day that goes by when the two of us don't make contact. This small daily injection of phoebe into our awareness is vital to our well-being. The phoebes give us a great deal of pleasure and a firsthand education in natural history. They provide us with an optimism: even though the swallows no longer return to Capistrano,* the phoebes still return to Irvington, New York. Which means that, year after year, as they journey to and from their wintering grounds in Mexico or the South, the phoebes have found adequate shelter and sustenance while not ingesting any toxins that will kill them or affect their ability to raise their young. Which means that every tree and shrub south of Irvington hasn't been leveled to the ground and that most of the water and soil are still relatively free of pesticides and herbicides. A lot is resting on the return of the phoebes to our backyard each spring and the logging of them in our backyard journal. "Hallelujah, the phoebes are back."

In Search of a Journal

I began to keep my Backyard List on scraps of paper that were intended to be transferred to a main list. When the list evolved into a journal I resorted to a spiral notebook. But I wanted something better, something more appropriate, something more substantial. The very nature of the Backyard List conjures up its own book, its own format. It wouldn't be filed away with the other lists. It could be left out on the coffee table, fireplace mantle, or desk, accessible for anyone to browse through or make an entry in. In this journal you could record at whim or with purpose a natural history of your home.

---

*Swallows have historically, every spring, returned to Mission San Juan Capistrano in California, where they build or repair old nests on the mission walls and soon after breed. The town of Capistrano would always celebrate the Festival of the Swallows with the return of the swallows; thousands of people came to witness the event. Today, the swallows no longer return to the mission. Swallows feed on insects they catch over open fields and meadows. The town of Capistrano lost its open fields and meadows to real estate development, and soon the mission of Capistrano lost its swallows.

PUTTING YOUR JOURNAL TO USE

A BACKYARD is as far as you can see, up into the sky and down the road or street. It is the total acreage of your property, and if you can see your neighbor's property, his as well. It could be a lawn, meadow, marsh, shoreline, ocean, forest, or the mountains. It could be a view from your summer home in the country or at the shore. It could be a view from your apartment window. Home is the criterion; all you have to do is make it home and what you see from it is your backyard. The difference between one backyard and another, and which will draw the greater number of birds, lies in the quality of habitat, the food sources, migration routes, and time of the year.

A comment about birding in cities: Excluding penthouses, court-yard gardens, and urban backyards, the prospects seem bleak; nevertheless I had a small but rewarding Backyard List from my apartment window in Chicago. My window faced a tall old maple tree. All I needed was that tree and one good spring migration. I've seen Black-throated Green Warblers, Black-and-white warblers, Blackpoll Warblers, Yellow-rumped Warblers, Brown Creepers, and Golden-crowned and Ruby-crowned Kinglets, to mention most but not all. During the spring and summer I have seen Purple Martins, Night-hawks, and Chimney Swifts feeding on the wing. If you should happen to work in San Francisco, and have your office window facing Golden Gate Park, you could rack up over ninety species throughout the year and still get your job done.

Most of us will identify the majority of our backyard birds by sight. To remove any doubt on what constitutes a legitimate entry for the Backyard List I mention the following: identifying a bird by its song or call alone qualifies that bird for the Backyard List; identifying a bird's song goes along with the territory—it's part of the skills a birder acquires. There are birders who can sit in their backyard at night and identify the calls of migratory birds as they fly over. It is possible for a birder who is blind to identify as many birds as a birder who has sight; birds fly and sing, carrying their identity not only in their form and feathers, but also in their voice.

The Backyard Birder's Journal is designed so you can keep a daily, monthly, and seasonal Backyard List. Each day has space to record the day's date, your daily list and observations. There are two days per journal page. If you have an exceptionally big day in your back-yard, culminating in a big list that needs more space than is allotted for one day, or if you need more space for comments and observations, just keep on writing into the following days' space.

How active you and your backyard birds are will determine how quickly you will fill up the pages of your journal. Once you end a year in December, even if you haven't logged in all of the pages, you'll record January birds for the new year in the same section you entered last January's birds. This will give you the opportunity of comparing, at a glance, the arrival and departure dates, species seen, weather conditions, or any other conditions, comments, and observations with those from previous years. There's much to learn and enjoy from the comparison of these simple data.

The Backyard List is subject to all the other categories a birder's list keeping has gone through. In your journal there are special sections where you can record your Backyard Life List, Backyard Big Year, Backyard Big Day, Backyard Nesting Birds, Backyard Christmas Count, and Backyard Rarities. Take advantage of these categories—use them. They'll provide you with a yearly overview of the avian goings-on in your backyard; they are easy to tabulate and are a pleasure to review and ponder.

A Backyard Big Year is a total record of the species of birds you have seen in your backyard in one calendar year. The total number will change from year to year, depending on how much time you put in and what kind of spring and fall migrations you are experiencing. The keeping of this list could provide you with a lifelong and pressureless challenge—it's a record you could try to top every year.

A Backyard Big Day is best attempted during the height of spring or fall migration. Pick a day when the weather conditions look favorable, and then devote several hours in the morning, afternoon, and evening for ferreting out your backyard birds; leave no corner, vista, shrub, tree, nook, or cranny untouched by your binoculars. If you have the time and inclination, you can try for several big days in one season.

Your Backyard Life List is a record of every species of bird you have identified in your backyard; it is an ongoing list. When you first begin to keep your Backyard Life List it will fill up rapidly. Often,

after six to ten years of birding in the same backyard, your Backyard Life List will seem to have neared its saturation point. How many species can one individual squeeze out of one backyard after so many years of birding in it? You'd be surprised. There's always the possibility for one more new bird. The quality of habitat, the migration routes, the ability and persistence of the individual, and the fact that your home is where you consistently spend a good deal of time are factors that will help contribute a new species to a seemingly loaded Backyard Life List. I have birded for over eight years in my backyard and have seen many of the species that are likely to come through; nevertheless, a new bird will eventually turn up; that new bird, at this stage of the game, always proves to be very exciting. So never say your Backyard Life List is over until you pick up and change residence. And then you can look forward to starting your Backyard Life List all over again.

Other printed formats for other lists birders keep are normally filed away. Your *Backyard Birder's Journal* should be kept out or made easily accessible for entry or reference. You never know when a new backyard bird might present itself, when a migratory wave might hit, or when you and your resident birds might cross paths, maybe giving you an entire new perspective on what those birds are all about. Your *Backyard Birder's Journal* can be your own personal journal, kept only by you, or it can be kept by all interested members of the family; it's a wonderful experience to share with children. Your five-year-old, along with you, can discover and log a bird into the journal. When you go out of town for a week, ask your eleven-year-old daughter or son to keep the journal until you get back.

As I've said before, the Backyard List has a heart; it has possibilities. It can be anything you make it. It can be a record of your backyard birds—a record of your resident, migratory, nesting, and winter birds. This simple list alone is involving and satisfying. You can invent other variations on the Backyard List. Lawrence Binford, with an impressive Backyard Life List of 147 species seen over thirty-three years from his backyard in Glencoe, Illinois, has devised and kept an equally impressive Birdbath List: 57 species of birds have soaked, fluttered about, bathed in, and drunk from his four-foot round birdbath. The Backyard List provides challenge if one wants to perceive it that way; there's always last year's Backyard Big Year or last year's Backyard Big Day to beat, and there's always the Backyard Life List to add to. Your *Backyard Birder's Journal* can also be a record of a bird's behavior, and a record of your and your family's reaction to that behavior. As time passes, your backyard journal will become more valuable, more pertinent; it can be read as a yearly record of the changes and events of the avifauna in your backyard and of the changes and events of your family and home as well.

After you spend some time at backyard birding and list keeping, I'd like to know how and what your backyard birds are doing. Who are your resident, migratory, nesting, and wintering birds? What unusual birds have you seen in your backyard, in your part of the country? And I wouldn't mind reading over your Backyard Life List. Write me in care of the publisher when you have the time and inclination. I'd be pleased to hear from you.

THE JOURNAL

The Seasons Pervade

WHAT TO EXPECT IN YOUR BACKYARD AND WHEN

OVERALL YEARLY temperatures and moisture, collectively called climate, are responsible for the nature of the landscape and, in turn, the nature of the avian populations that inhabit the landscape. A backyard in the foothills of New Mexico differs in plant and bird life from a backyard along the Hudson River in New York. Each logs in its own unique backyard bird list, but in spite of their differences each has a bird or two in common, and as temperature and daylight increase and decrease, each backyard will go through its seasonal paces.

Depending on what time of year they are present and what they are doing, your backyard birds fall into certain recognizable categories.

Permanent Residents (PR). These birds remain in or near your backyard all year round and do not migrate.

Summer Residents (SR). These birds travel from their southern wintering grounds northward each spring to nest in or near your backyard. They'll spend the summer and fly south come fall.

Winter Residents (WR). Some birds fly to South America to reach their southern wintering grounds. Others winter no farther south than your backyard—they are your winter residents. They arrive in the fall from farther north, spend the winter, and fly back come spring.

Migratory Transients (MT). These birds pass through your backyard during their northern and southern migrations each spring (MT-Sp) or fall (MT-Fa).

Nesting (N). This label helps define your permanent and summer residents. If you are sure one of them is nesting in your backyard it may be described as a permanent resident–nesting (PR-N) or summer resident–nesting (SR-N). If you are not sure, drop the N.

Occasional (O). Every few years the same species may pass through your backyard as a spring (MT-OSp) or fall (MT-OFa) migrant. Or it might stop off as a summer or winter visitor. The category *visitor* implies occasional. A winter (WV) or summer (SV) visitor can appear anytime during a season. You might see one of them or a small flock. You might see them for one day or a month and then not see them again until a year, two years, or six years later. They are sporadic in their appearance. Also, permanent residents are sometimes known to be permanent in your locale but will not always be seen in your backyard; they come through periodically throughout the year or years and can be annointed permanent resident–occasional (PR-O).

Rare (Ra). The bird isn't supposed to be in your backyard, county, state, or maybe even the country. A rare species is one that has never been sighted in your region or has not been seen very often.

Note that a bird rare for your backyard may not be rare for your area; continued birding from your backyard could prove the bird to be an occasional visitor or occasional migrant; check your field guide's range maps and regional state guides for a bird's distribution.

Vertical Migrant (VM). Vertical migration is when a bird migrates from one altitude to another: in the spring to higher altitudes to breed, in the fall to lower altitudes to spend the winter. Vertical migration is explained further in the section on spring.

No Longer Seen (NLS). Applied to resident birds or regular migrants that have disappeared from your backyard.

Overhead (OV). Birds seen flying over your backyard and showing no interest in landing.

These categories provide you with a way to see and think about your backyard birds. In keeping your own backyard list, use these as you see fit or come up with your own.

To help illustrate the similarities and differences between backyards in the seasonal sections that follow, I have arbitrarily selected five backyards from different parts of the country, my own included. Each backyard has its own particular shrubs, trees, gardens, and size of lawn appealing to its human and avian occupants. Several are edged with woodlot and wild shrub, one is located in a semiarid suburb, while another is a small ornamental urban garden packed in among other urban gardens. However they differ, they all provide for the birds. In each seasonal section you'll get a chance to meet their permanent, summer, and winter residents, their nesting birds, and their spring and fall migrants. Each seasonal backyard bird list represents birds seen throughout the years. They are not a final tabulation. They are not a static record. They are ongoing lists, increasing over the years, and by the time you read them they will have changed. Following is a brief description of each individual backyard:

its flora, surroundings, and peculiarities, and the total number of species making up each individual's Backyard Life List.

THE BLUMES' BACKYARD
SUBURBAN   *Irvington, New York*

That's my backyard. It's a little over four acres, one of which is lawn, ornamental shrubs, and ground cover. The rest is a small woodlot edged with prickly brambles and other wild shrubs. The woodlot consists of white and black oak, red and sugar maple, gray birch, yellow poplar, white and green ash, black cherry, and invading hordes of ailanthus (tree of heaven).

There is a nearby pond. My neighbors all have similar yards with lawn and woodlot and are all up on a ridge surrounded by roads and an expressway, three miles from the Hudson River.

I have two hanging feeders filled with wild bird seed and often supplemented with sunflower seed.

My Backyard Life List numbers 103 species.

THE GUDASES' BACKYARD
SUBURBAN   *Baton Rouge, Louisiana*

Almena Gudas's backyard is approximately 100 feet wide by 200 feet deep. Most of the lots in her subdivision are similar in size and landscaping. The backyards are bordered on each side by tall, thick shrubs and trees: azalea, privet, and mock orange, along with red, white, and pin oak, elm, magnolia, yellow poplar, dogwood, buckeye, and ironwood. At the rear is a wooded strip that is left on its own and that creates the prolific "edge" that attracts a number of birds (see Backyard as Habitat).

Almena has two standing feeders and two hanging feeders filled with sunflower seed, wild bird seed mix, and chicken scratch. She has several hummingbird feeders. During the cold months she puts out suet.

Almena's Backyard Life List numbers 77 species.

THE WILLIAMSES' BACKYARD
SUBURBAN   *Silver City, New Mexico*

Harvey Williams's backyard is two acres and, like his neighbors' backyards, consists mostly of native plants: pinyon, oak, juniper, squawbush, and mountain mahogany. Ponderosa pine has been reintroduced, along with Russian olive and pyracantha.

Harvey's backyard is semiarid, 6050 feet up, putting it, as he describes, "in the transitional zone between upper Sonoran and the firaspen belt." Thus, the backyard is subject not only to north-south-axis spring and fall migrations but also to the phenomenon of vertical migration, discussed later under Spring.

Harvey has post-mounted and hanging feeders. His feed is mostly whole milo and mixed grains. He also has extensive hummingbird feeders with uncolored sugar water. Water is extremely important, especially in the summer months, and he supplies it throughout the year.

Harvey Williams's Backyard Life List numbers 95 species.

THE KILLPACKS' BACKYARD
SUBURBAN   *Ogden, Utah*

Merlin Killpack's backyard is an 85-by-140-foot lot, edged with Gambel's oak, wild currant, pyracantha, lilac, multiflora rose, and honeysuckle. It also claims apple, pear, apricot, plum, and cherry trees and an English soft-shelled walnut. Some of his neighbors' backyards are similar to Merlin's, and some are, as Merlin puts it, "pushing for a clean-polished main-street-type yard." What make Merlin's and his neighbors' yards unusual and give them all scope are the adjoining foothills and mountains, a hundred yards off and by definition part of his backyard.

Merlin feeds his birds year round. He uses cracked corn mixed with wheat and milo, sunflower seeds, and wild bird seed mixes.

An important aspect of Merlin Killpack's backyard birding is bird banding. He's a hands-on birder, gathering up birds as he would pluck apples from his apple tree. Interrupting a bird's flight by means of a fine, delicate "mist net" stretched across an opening in the trees or shrubs, Merlin will carefully take it out of the net. If the bird hasn't already been banded, he places an appropriate-sized band made of aluminum alloy around the shank of the bird: he notes its species, the serial number of its band, the place and date of its banding, the bird's age and sex, whether it's an adult or immature, and its general condition. He then releases the bird and sends the information off to the Bird Banding Laboratory in Laurel, Maryland. Bird banding gives us information about the range of a bird, its life span, and its nesting and wintering grounds. It tell us of a bird's propensity and ability to return year after year to the same forest, meadow, marsh, or backyard. And it keeps Merlin Killpack in close touch with his backyard birds.

Merlin Killpack's Backyard Life List numbers 88 species.

THE MURPHYS' BACKYARD
URBAN   *San Francisco, California*

Dan Murphy's backyard, along with most of San Francisco's residential neighborhoods, presents a slightly offbeat picture, especially to an easterner like myself. Dan's and his neighbors' homes are deliberately arranged to line up with each other along their front edges, with the sides touching or almost touching—presenting, as Dan tells it, a united front to resist attack from foreign invaders from the sea.

Subsequently, each backyard runs continuous with the next, only separated by fences. Dan's backyard is a 40-by-30-foot lot with lawn, ornamental shrubs, flower beds, and fish pond. His adjoining neighbors' yards vary from manicured to weeds to concrete.

There are nearby parks and enclosed reservoirs—a phenomenon I am unaccustomed to: all the reservoirs I've seen out East present a surface available for bird or man to fish from. The reservoirs in San Francisco are covered with blacktop—a sea of blacktop. But all is not lost, because the blacktop is decorated with thousands of gulls and hundreds of plovers standing stiff legged into the wind or plopped down on their bellies resting.

I mention the gulls and plovers because they are part of the traffic flying over Dan's backyard. Dan's yard is located between Lake Merced and the Pacific Ocean, putting him in a traffic pattern of waterbirds flying back and forth from one body of water to another. Dan has become sensitive to this overhead traffic and has devised the classification Overhead to distinguish those birds seen flying over his backyard from those seen in it.

One other peculiarity I should mention. The backyard birding in San Francisco is not quite in synch with most of the country. Spring migrants are on the move in February, and by early June the nesting season is over.

Dan has one feeder filled with mixed seed. He weans the birds from the feeder by reducing feed during mid-March. He continually reduces the feed until the second week in April, when he stops feeding altogether. He resumes feeding by the second week in October. Dan also has one hummingbird feeder and one large terra-cotta flowerpot for water.

Dan's Backyard Life List numbers 51 species.

WINTER

DECEMBER·JANUARY·FEBRUARY

IF DECEMBER reminds us once again what cold temperatures feel like, January won't let us forget. So once you commit to feeding your backyard birds, stay committed. By December you will have built up a loyal following: your permanent residents, your winter residents, and maybe a few lingerers.

Lingerers are birds that usually head south for the winter; but because of your hospitality and possibly because of a run of unusually mild weather they decide to stay on. There is a good chance that if they're with you by mid-December they're with you all winter.

Your backyard may also be the recipient of an irruption. Birds that normally live year round in parts of Canada and Alaska pick up en masse during the fall and winter and move south. An irruption occurs when a particular species' population is up and their natural food supply is down. Those with a reputation for flooding southward are Pine Grosbeaks, Evening Grosbeaks, Purple Finches, Red and White Crossbills, Hoary and Common Redpolls, Pine Siskins, Bohemian Waxwings, Snowy Owls, and Great Gray Owls. One of them may turn up at your feeder.

If there is anything left of the fall migration it will end in early December. Waterfowl are the exception for they're apt to continue on through the month.

For those of you who are fortunate enough to have your home overlooking open water (ocean, river, lake, bay, or pond), December, January, and February will bring you wintering ducks, gulls, and other waterbirds.

With the aid of my scope, from my apartment window overlooking Chicago's Lake Michigan I saw Common Goldeneyes, Oldsquaws, Greater and Lesser Scaups, Ring-necked Ducks, White-winged Scoters, Common Mergansers, and Red-breasted Mergansers. An ornithologist friend who lived in an apartment overlooking the Hudson River in Cold Spring, New York, saw most of what I saw in Lake Michigan, including Hooded Mergansers, Ruddy Ducks, Buffleheads, Canvasbacks, Double-crested Cormorants, Canada Geese, Mute Swans, Belted Kingfishers, and Great Blue Herons—the latter two unlikely for the middle of the winter, but so.

The end of February might bring you a hint of the coming spring migration in the form of an early robin, grackle, or Red-winged Blackbird. Or, then again, it might bring you more of February.

The Backyard Christmas Count

Make a Christmas Count in your own backyard. Since backyards are usually limited in size you might make your Backyard Christmas

Count more interesting if, instead of selecting one day, you recorded your backyard birds for the entire week of Christmas.

Or participate—volunteer your backyard for the annual Christmas Count in your locale. You can never tell how important your backyard data might be. In the 1985 Christmas Count in Oakland, California, the only White-throated Sparrow was found at a feeder.

Increasing Activity Around the Feeder—An Exercise in Seeing

We gather around the feeder to watch birds gathering around the feeder—a symbiotic relationship, all our doing. The birds don't need us—we need them. Their availability helps us get through the short, cold winter days much like TV, cross-country skiing, and wood-burning stoves do. They provide us with a basic diversion, the diversion of staring, which can be carried to a satisfying extreme. Look at a bird. Take a really good long look. It is easier for a bright red cardinal to get a response from humankind than a drab, nondescript gray junco. Now we can spend some of our time at the feeder delving not only into the brilliant reds of a cardinal but into the rich, subtle grays of a junco.

By noticing the details you will begin to appreciate the subtleties. If you look closely at a junco you will see shades of gray, graded by the changing daylight. In profile, the frosted pink triangular bill is tangent to a deep slate gray head; head-on, the pink bill is set into a blackish center, surrounded by a rich field of gray. The white belly is outlined by bold gray strokes; the eyes are two black, polished pebbles hidden in the deep gray of the head. A bird's form can be thought of as a warm-blooded canvas rendered with a limited palette and by random genetic adjustments allowed to reproduce, resulting in junco,

cardinal, titmouse, and reflecting an innate understanding and execution of esthetics. An artist might use the same palette, might make the same statement—the junco statement. The titmouse statement is a brush of orange flank separating a white belly from a gray wing, black eyes protruding pop-eyed from a field of white cheek, topped with an erect gray crest. The Tufted Titmouse is a beautiful and unique-looking soft, warm midgray bird, but only upon a closer look.

So, in these cold winter months, take time out to relax and meditate on the details—the yellow lores of a White-throated Sparrow or the yellow crown of a Golden-crowned Sparrow. Scrutinize the design of a Pine Siskin, Tree Sparrow, or any of your winter or permanent residents at the feeder. Learn to see and articulate a bird's nomenclature. Carefully describe to yourself a bird's eye, bill, and leg color; eye ring and eye line; primaries and secondaries; wing bars and wing coverts; crown and breast; flank and rump—and as you scrutinize and articulate a bird's color and field marks you will, in effect, be in training, sharpening up your eye for the coming spring migration and developing your birding skills.

Sharing Your Backyard Data

Every February the Annual Bird Feeding Census surveys the status of bird populations at the feeders throughout the United States. If you want to participate in the census, note the names and numbers of the species frequenting the immediate area around your feeder throughout the month of February and send this information to the Bird Feeders Society, P.O. Box 243, Mystic, CT 06355. Findings are reported in the Bird Feeders Society quarterly publication, *Around the Bird Feeder*. They accept membership.

THE BLUMES' WINTER BACKYARD BIRD LIST
SUBURBAN   *Irvington, New York*

Permanent Residents. Canada Goose—OV, Red-tailed Hawk, Ring-billed Gull—OV, Herring Gull—OV, Mourning Dove, Eastern Screech-Owl—O, Downy Woodpecker, Hairy Woodpecker, Pileated Woodpecker—O, Blue Jay, American Crow, Black-capped Chickadee, Tufted Titmouse, White-breasted Nuthatch, Northern Mockingbird, Cedar Waxwing—O, European Starling, Northern Cardinal, Song Sparrow, House Finch, American Goldfinch, House Sparrow.
  Winter Residents. American Tree Sparrow—O, White-throated Sparrow, Dark-eyed (Slate-colored) Junco, Pine Siskin—O.
  Winter Visitors. Sharp-shinned Hawk—O, Red-bellied Woodpecker, Red-breasted Nuthatch—O, Brown Creeper, Golden-crowned Kinglet, Rufous-sided Towhee—O, Fox Sparrow—O, Red-winged Blackbird—O, Common Redpoll—Ra, Evening Grosbeak—O.

Observations and Comments by Howard Blume

January 15, 1981.   "Ten above zero. A big warm smile on my face. Eight Common Redpolls at the feeder. The last time I saw redpolls was twelve years ago, in below-zero weather at a frozen-over marsh on the outskirts of Chicago."

February 21, 1984.   "Kay and I soak in the hot tub, watching the chickadees and titmouses fly back and forth to the feeder. Suddenly a Sharp-shinned Hawk nabs a titmouse in midflight and carries it off to perch on one of the poles to the stockade fence. I think I can see the sunflower seed still gripped in the titmouse's upper and lower mandibles."

THE GUDASES' WINTER BACKYARD BIRD LIST
SUBURBAN   *Baton Rouge, Louisiana*

Permanent Residents. Wood Duck, Mourning Dove, Barred Owl, Red-headed Woodpecker, Red-bellied Woodpecker, Downy Woodpecker, Hairy Woodpecker, Northern Flicker, Pileated Woodpecker—NLS, Blue Jay, American Crow, Carolina Chickadee, Tufted Titmouse, Carolina Wren, Eastern Bluebird, Northern Mockingbird, Brown Thrasher, European Starling, Pine Warbler, Northern Cardinal, Rufous-sided Towhee, Chipping Sparrow, Field Sparrow, Red-winged Blackbird, Common Grackle, Brown-headed Cowbird, House Sparrow.
  Winter Residents. Yellow-bellied Sapsucker, Eastern Phoebe, Ruby-crowned Kinglet, Hermit Thrush, Orange-crowned Warbler, Yellow-rumped Warbler, White-throated Sparrow.
  Winter Visitors. Rufous Hummingbird—O, Bewick's Wren, House Wren, Winter Wren, American Robin, Cedar Waxwing, Rose-breasted Grosbeak—Ra, Black-headed Grosbeak—Ra, Dark-eyed Junco, Rusty Blackbird, Brewer's Blackbird, Purple Finch, Pine Siskin—O, American Goldfinch, Evening Grosbeak—O.

Observations and Comments by Almena P. Gudas

"Since our climate is variable and migrations seem to vary from year to year, we never know what will appear in the winter months. Our most exciting winters were 1968–69, 1972–73, and 1977–78, when we had large flocks of Evening Grosbeaks that do not normally winter here.
  "January 30 this year [1986] a Black-headed Grosbeak made an appearance in our backyard. It stayed around for several weeks.

Three graduate students from Louisiana State came by to look at the bird. A total of 66 individuals have been seen in the state. And that record was only kept up to the year 1970."

THE WILLIAMSES' WINTER BACKYARD BIRD LIST
SUBURBAN   *Silver City, New Mexico*

Permanent Residents. Northern Harrier—O, Sharp-shinned Hawk—O, Cooper's Hawk, Red-tailed Hawk, Golden Eagle—O, American Kestrel, Gambel's Quail, Killdeer—O, Mourning Dove, Greater Roadrunner, Western Screech-Owl—O, Great Horned Owl, Acorn Woodpecker, Yellow-bellied Sapsucker—O, Williamson's Sapsucker, Ladder-backed Woodpecker, Downy Woodpecker—O, Hairy Woodpecker, Northern Flicker, Say's Phoebe—O, Vermilion Flycatcher—O, Steller's Jay—O, Scrub Jay, American Crow—O, Common Raven, Plain Titmouse, Bushtit, Bewick's Wren, Western Bluebird, Townsend's Solitaire, Curve-billed Thrasher, Cedar Waxwing—O, Phainopepla—O, Loggerhead Shrike—O, Rufous-sided Towhee, Brown Towhee, House Finch.
Winter Residents. White-breasted Nuthatch, White-crowned Sparrow, Dark-eyed (Oregon, Gray-headed) Junco.
Winter Visitors. Mountain Chickadee—O-VM, Bridled Titmouse—O-VM, Red-breasted Nuthatch—O-VM, Brown Creeper—O-VM, Ruby-crowned Kinglet, American Robin, Rufous-crowned Sparrow.

Observations and Comments by Harvey Williams

December.   "Continued pleasant days, cold nights, chance of light snow. Winter birds are in place and stable."

January.   "Most severe winter month. Bird populations quite stable. Occasional moderate snow makes scatter feeding necessary."

February.   "Less severe weather. Raptors pair off and start to refurbish existing nests. Great Horned Owls mate."

THE KILLPACKS' WINTER BACKYARD BIRD LIST
SUBURBAN   *Ogden, Utah*

Permanent Residents. Golden Eagle—O, American Kestrel—O, Chukar—O, Northern (Red-shafted) Flicker, Scrub Jay, Black-billed Magpie, Black-capped Chickadee, Blue-gray Gnatcatcher, American Robin, Cedar Waxwing—O, European Starling, Rufous-sided Towhee, Pine Siskin—O, American Goldfinch—O.
Winter Residents. Sharp-shinned Hawk, Downy Woodpecker, Mountain Chickadee, Ruby-crowned Kinglet, Townsend's Solitaire, Bohemian Waxwing, White-crowned Sparrow, Dark-eyed (Slate-colored—O, Pink-sided, Gray-headed) Junco.
Winter Visitors. Northern Goshawk—O, Ring-necked Pheasant—O, Ruffed Grouse—Ra, California Quail, Steller's Jay—O, Red-breasted Nuthatch—O, Northern Shrike—Ra, Harris' Sparrow—Ra, Cassin's Finch—O, Evening Grosbeak—O.

Observations and Comments by Merlin Killpack

December.   "Sometimes snow, sometimes a milder period. Winter birds are gathering at feeders and berries of pyracantha, Russian olive, and honeysuckle. We see an occasional Townsend's Solitaire."

January. "Usually below freezing, snow on the ground, and winter residents present, like Dark-eyed Juncos with varieties (Slate-colored and Pink-sided)."

"There were very few Pine Siskins several years ago; a large flock this year all winter—over 1000 individuals. Banded over 700 and still a lot in yard without bands. There are usually a few all winter, then they increase in April and May and then disappear for nesting."

THE MURPHYS' WINTER BACKYARD BIRD LIST
URBAN *San Francisco, California*

Permanent Residents. California Quail—Sp, Killdeer—OV, Rock Dove, Mourning Dove, Anna's Hummingbird, American Crow—O-OV, Common Raven—OV, Chestnut-backed Chickadee, Bushtit, American Robin, Northern Mockingbird—Sp, Fa, European Starling, Brown Towhee, White-crowned Sparrow, Brewer's Blackbird, Brown-headed Cowbird, House Finch, Lesser Goldfinch, House Sparrow.

Winter Residents. Double-crested Cormorant—OV, Mallard—OV, American Wigeon—OV, Mew Gull—OV, California Gull—OV, Glaucous-winged Gull—OV, Northern (Red-shafted) Flicker, Ruby-crowned Kinglet, Cedar Waxwing, Yellow-rumped Warbler, Golden-crowned Sparrow, Dark-eyed (Oregon) Junco, Pine Siskin, American Goldfinch.

Winter Visitors. Sharp-shinned Hawk—O, Cooper's Hawk—O, American Kestrel—O, Band-tailed Pigeon, Black Phoebe, Red-winged Blackbird, Red Crossbill—Ra.

Observations and Comments by Dan Murphy

December. "Kestrels, Sharp-shinned and Cooper's Hawks discover the benefits of the feeder." [What Dan is referring to are the birds feeding at the feeder, which become feed for the predator hawks.]

February. "Allen's Hummingbird migration by middle of month. They establish territories by end of month. Swallow migration in full swing." [Throughout most of the country there will be very few signs of a spring migration, if any. For the sake of continuity we include Dan's migration list in the section on spring.]

December

DATE

DATE

December

DATE

DATE

December

DATE _____

_____
_____
_____
_____
_____
_____
_____
_____
_____
_____

DATE _____

_____
_____
_____
_____
_____
_____
_____
_____
_____
_____

December

DATE _____

_____

_____

_____

_____

_____

_____

_____

_____

_____

_____

DATE _____

_____

_____

_____

_____

_____

_____

_____

_____

_____

_____

December

DATE

DATE

December

DATE

DATE

December

DATE _____

_____
_____
_____
_____
_____
_____
_____
_____
_____
_____
_____
_____

DATE _____

_____
_____
_____
_____
_____
_____
_____
_____
_____
_____
_____
_____

December

DATE _____

_____
_____
_____
_____
_____
_____
_____
_____
_____
_____
_____

DATE _____

_____
_____
_____
_____
_____
_____
_____
_____
_____
_____
_____

December

DATE

DATE

December

DATE

DATE

December

DATE

DATE

December

DATE _____

_____

_____

_____

_____

_____

_____

_____

_____

_____

DATE _____

_____

_____

_____

_____

_____

_____

_____

_____

_____

December

DATE

DATE

December

DATE _____

DATE _____

December

DATE

DATE

December

DATE _____

_____
_____
_____
_____
_____
_____
_____
_____
_____
_____
_____
_____

DATE _____

_____
_____
_____
_____
_____
_____
_____
_____
_____
_____
_____
_____

January

DATE

DATE

January

DATE _____

_____

_____

_____

_____

_____

_____

_____

_____

_____

_____

_____

DATE _____

_____

_____

_____

_____

_____

_____

_____

_____

_____

_____

_____

January

DATE

DATE

January

DATE

DATE

January

DATE

DATE

January

DATE

DATE

January

DATE

DATE

January

DATE

DATE

January

DATE

DATE

January

DATE _____

_____

_____

_____

_____

_____

_____

_____

_____

_____

_____

DATE _____

_____

_____

_____

_____

_____

_____

_____

_____

_____

_____

January

DATE

DATE

January

DATE _____

DATE _____

January

DATE

DATE

January

DATE _____

_____

_____

_____

_____

_____

_____

_____

_____

_____

_____

_____

_____

DATE _____

_____

_____

_____

_____

_____

_____

_____

_____

_____

_____

_____

_____

January

DATE

DATE

January

DATE

DATE

February

DATE

DATE

February

DATE _____

_____
_____
_____
_____
_____
_____
_____
_____
_____
_____
_____

DATE _____

_____
_____
_____
_____
_____
_____
_____
_____
_____
_____
_____

February

DATE

DATE

February

DATE

DATE

February

DATE _____

_____

_____

_____

_____

_____

_____

_____

_____

_____

_____

DATE _____

_____

_____

_____

_____

_____

_____

_____

_____

_____

_____

February

DATE

DATE

February

DATE _____

_____

_____

_____

_____

_____

_____

_____

_____

_____

_____

_____

DATE _____

_____

_____

_____

_____

_____

_____

_____

_____

_____

_____

_____

February

DATE _____

DATE _____

February

DATE

DATE

February

DATE

DATE

February

DATE _____

_____

_____

_____

_____

_____

_____

_____

_____

_____

_____

DATE _____

_____

_____

_____

_____

_____

_____

_____

_____

_____

_____

February

DATE _____

_____
_____
_____
_____
_____
_____
_____
_____
_____
_____
_____

DATE _____

_____
_____
_____
_____
_____
_____
_____
_____
_____
_____
_____

February

DATE

DATE

February

DATE _____

_____
_____
_____
_____
_____
_____
_____
_____
_____
_____
_____

DATE _____

_____
_____
_____
_____
_____
_____
_____
_____
_____
_____
_____

February

DATE

DATE

February

DATE

DATE

SPRING

MARCH · APRIL · MAY

IF THE END of February hasn't offered a hint of the oncoming spring migration, March will. One cold, bleak March morning, maybe as you're taking out the garbage, a sudden appearance of a Red-winged Blackbird and its hoarse, melodic song will pick up where winter's old songs wane; if not a Red-wing, then an Eastern or Say's Phoebe; if not a phoebe, then some other migratory vanguard common to your part of the country. By the end of March your permanent and winter residents will have changed their song.

By April the birds will decidedly be on the move. Winter residents will be leaving your backyard to fly north, answering their own call, their own time and place. If a beach is part of your backyard, check out the shorebirds; they'll be showing up along the shore and mud flats, especially after bad weather. If your backyard overlooks a lake or pond with an adjoining marsh, consider yourself fortunate and watch out for herons, rails, snipe, and sandpipers. Waterfowl will be peaking. Check out the skys for flights of hawks, gulls, swifts, and swallows.

The sky swarms with miraculous stunts: Ruby-throated Hummingbirds, weighing one-eighth of an ounce, fly five hundred miles over the Gulf of Mexico, wings beating fifty times a second for twenty-five continuous hours. And that's not even the half of it. Once the Ruby-throats reach land, they have all kinds of choices: after they replenish their body fat they can stay on to nest in Florida, Alabama, Mississippi, or Almena P. Gudas's backyard in Baton Rouge, Louisiana, or they can push on farther north, some remaining at various points along the way to nest and some reaching their northernmost nesting grounds in Canada and Nova Scotia.

April brings the first waves of wrens, kinglets, thrushes, warblers, and sparrows. Backyards become alive with new green shoots and leaves, the energy of birds, their chatter, their flutters, their purpose—to nest, to mate, to incubate eggs, and to raise broods.

All bird-dom breaks loose in May—the height of the migration. Give yourself plenty of lead time on your way through your backyard wherever you're going; you're going to need it. Distraction will abound in the form of flycatchers, thrashers, warblers, thrushes, tanagers, orioles, and more. They will be in full breeding plumage, which means they will never look as good, and they will be in top voice. If a wave of warblers takes respite in your backyard, you'll know; all you have to do is listen.

Bird Songs

Early in March would be a good time for you to pick up a tape or record of bird songs and begin to learn or review the songs of those birds that will be migrating to and through your backyard.

Knowing a species' song only adds to your pleasure. Imagine: There you are, one early May morning lying in bed half awake. You hear the mix of buzzings and melodious songs coming from outside your open window. While your head is still on the pillow you begin to sort them out. After a couple of minutes you know that waiting for you outside in that big old maple tree are a pair of Rose-breasted Grosbeaks, a Northern Oriole, more than one Northern Parula, and maybe—you're not sure, you'll have to check it out—a Chestnut-sided Warbler. That's not such a bad way to get out of bed—knowing what has recently arrived and what is waiting for your perusal outside in your backyard.

An excellent recording of bird songs is Peterson's *A Field Guide to Bird Song.* One album or cassette covers eastern and central North America; another covers western bird songs.

The Weather

Flying is a lot easier going with the wind, so look out for southerly winds—they could be carrying your next wave of migrating birds. This rule applies to most of the country but especially to the eastern United States, where southerly winds carrying a warm, moist mass of air from the Gulf of Mexico or the Caribbean can kick off a wave of migrating birds.

Also pay attention to a south-moving cold front. If it meets that southern warm mass of air it stops the birds cold; they're forced to land—in your backyard if you're lucky.

Vertical Migration

Instead of migrating north and south, some birds migrate in elevations. This vertical, or longitudinal, migration takes place in the high western mountains of North America. In late fall and early winter the birds that live in the mountains descend to the lower slopes and valleys for milder weather as an equivalent for migrating south. In the spring the birds leave the lower altitudes to nest in the higher parts of the mountains—equivalent to migrating north.

For example, in early April, Mountain Quail, starting from elevations of 5000 feet or below, gather together in groups of 10 to 30 and walk single file up the mountainside to around 9500 feet to nest. Come fall, they form groups again and, single file, march back down.

Internal Rhythms in Migratory Birds

After a wave of migratory birds has made your day in your backyard, have you ever lain in bed later that night, tossing and turning, unable to sleep, asking yourself over and over again, how, how do they do it? How do birds know when it's time to migrate? Do birds take their cue from solar rhythms—the changing daylight and temperature we experience in our own backyards—or do they respond to internal rhythms—hormonal messages turned on by their own inner clock, regulated and coded by their own genetic program? Twenty years of insightful thinking and clever experiments have produced an answer, further questions, and a few more answers.

Researchers took their cue from birds who winter in equatorial Africa, where the length of daylight is fairly constant throughout the year. The length of daylight is known as the photoperiod, a term that often pops up among researchers who study bird migration. During the month of March every year, without external cue from a changing photoperiod, these equatorial wintering birds begin their migration north, giving a researcher strong reason to hypothesize that an internal cue triggered the move. Now to prove it.

Take a wild bird who is an experienced migrant. Place the bird in a cage and expose it to twelve hours of daylight, equatorial style: no seasonal variation for this bird—day after day, all year long, twelve hours of daylight. Take another wild bird, same species, cage it, and expose it to seasonal changes in daylight. Attach a microswitch to the perch in each cage and wire it to a recorder. When a bird hops on its perch, the hop will be recorded as a mark on a strip of paper. The more active a bird happens to be on its perch, the more marks. The birds used in this experiment were night migrants, and it was found that intensive hopping went on at night. A bird's hopping or hyperactivity, when sustained for a period of time, is called migratory restlessness, and for a very good reason.

Both birds exhibited migratory restlessness during the months of August and September and May and June—the fall and spring migrations. They both calmed down during December and January, going through their winter molts, as they would do on their wintering grounds. Since the caged bird that experienced no change in photoperiod still adhered to a normal schedule of migratory restlessness and molting, we can conclude that it responded to its own internal rhythms, known in the trade as endogenous rhythms.

What else can we glean from migratory restlessness? It was observed that under constant light and temperature, migratory restlessness and molting took slightly less than a year for a full cycle. The caged birds' winter molt took place every ten months, not the expected twelve, as it does in the wild. The "about a year" is called circannual, and birds undergoing seasonal deprivation demonstrate circannual rhythms. Birds in the wild are on an annual rhythm, being in synch with the solar year. So it was deduced that there had to be some external factor that brings a bird's circannual rhythm in synch with the solar year. And there is. When a caged bird is exposed to the seasonal variations of daylight that occur in the bird's breeding grounds, the bird's internal rhythm links up to the solar rhythm. So we have discovered that not only is a bird endowed with an internal

system that cues migratory restlessness and molting, but the system is flexible enough to adjust its own schedule to the environment. Is there no end to what we can learn from migratory restlessness?

Take the same species of bird we've been putting in cages, but this time, separate the young from their parents when they are a week old and raise them yourself. Take these hand-raised birds, cage them, and watch for migratory restlessness. It was discovered that these hand-raised, inexperienced birds, which never knew what it was to migrate, demonstrated migratory restlessness for the same amount of time it took for their wild counterparts to begin and finish migration. For instance: during fall migration the hand-raised caged birds' migratory restlessness began and subsided in approximately the same two months it took their wild counterparts to leave their breeding grounds and reach their winter home. The length of migratory restlessness was found to be proportional to the distance a bird migrates—which means that the distance a bird covers during migration is determined by an inner clock, triggering migratory restlessness and the beginning of migration; as soon as the inner clock stops, migratory restlessness subsides, and the bird's journey ends, on target, at its breeding or winter grounds.

Now, what a young bird needs to get it to its ancestral wintering grounds for the first time, besides its internal clock, which we now know cues the beginning and end of migration, is a means to choose the proper direction. Experiments show that a migrant's choice of compass heading can rely on the physical characteristics of the earth, the sun, the stars, and the earth's magnetic field. But can a bird's endogenous rhythms point it in the right direction?

Let's take our hand-raised bird, cage it, and eliminate all seasonal cues—no daylight, no night sky, leaving only the earth's magnetic field available. In the cage, our hand-raised bird will have eight perches to choose from—eight perches radiating out from a center point and representing eight different compass directions. Now, this particular species, when in the wild, heads southwest during the first leg of migration. On its second and last leg, the bird heads south. Our hand-raised bird spent the months of August and September hopping about in the southwest corner of the cage, and in November spent its migratory restlessness in the south corner, faithfully duplicating the compass directions of its wild counterpart. In the spring our hand-raised bird chose only the north perch, because in the wild it migrates due north, with no change of direction.

Now what happens if a young bird on its first migration to its wintering grounds is blown off course? Several researchers captured 11,000 starlings midway on their migratory route to their winter grounds in southern England and northern France. The researchers released the birds approximately five hundred miles off course, in Switzerland. The older birds, which had previously flown the migratory route, compensated for the displacement and flew toward their normal winter grounds. The younger birds flew the straight course called for by their inner compass and subsequently established a new winter range in southern France and the Iberian Peninsula.

Older birds who have migrated before can navigate over unknown regions and when displaced can find their way home. How they do it, no one yet knows. We'll have to wait while the ornithologists and zoologists ponder their caged birds and other phenomena, and in another twenty years or so they will again astound and enlighten us.

THE BLUMES' SPRING BACKYARD BIRD LIST
SUBURBAN   *Irvington, New York*

Permanent Residents. Canada Goose—OV, Red-tailed Hawk, Ring-billed Gull—OV, Herring Gull—OV, Mourning Dove, Eastern Screech-Owl—O, Downy Woodpecker, Hairy Woodpecker, Pileated Woodpecker—O, Blue Jay, American Crow, Black-capped Chickadee, Tufted Titmouse, White-breasted Nuthatch, Northern Mockingbird, Cedar Waxwing—O, European Starling, Northern Cardinal, Song Sparrow, House Finch, American Goldfinch, House Sparrow.

Migratory Transients. Yellow-billed Cuckoo—O, Ruby-throated Hummingbird, Yellow-bellied Sapsucker—O, Olive-sided Flycatcher—Ra, Eastern Wood-Pewee, Tree Swallow, Barn Swallow, Winter Wren, Gray-cheeked Thrush, Hermit Thrush, White-eyed Vireo, Solitary Vireo, Warbling Vireo, Nashville Warbler, Northern Parula, Yellow Warbler, Chestnut-sided Warbler, Magnolia Warbler, Cape May Warbler, Black-throated Blue Warbler, Yellow-rumped Warbler, Black-throated Green Warbler, Blackburnian Warbler, Prairie Warbler, Palm Warbler, Blackpoll Warbler, Cerulean Warbler, Black-and-white Warbler, American Redstart, Ovenbird, Mourning Warbler, Canada Warbler.

Summer Residents. Green-backed Heron, Wood Duck—O, Chimney Swift, Northern Flicker, Eastern Phoebe, Eastern Kingbird—O, House Wren, Veery, Swainson's Thrush—O, Wood Thrush, American Robin, Gray Catbird, Brown Thrasher—NLS, Red-eyed Vireo, Blue-winged Warbler, Yellow Warbler, Common Yellowthroat, Scarlet Tanager, Rose-breasted Grosbeak, Indigo Bunting, Rufous-sided Towhee, Red-winged Blackbird, Common Grackle, Brown-headed Cowbird, Northern Oriole.

Winter Residents. American Tree Sparrow—O, White-throated Sparrow, Dark-eyed (Slate-colored) Junco, Pine Siskin—O.

Observations and Comments by Howard Blume

May 1, 1981. "Lying on the floor doing sit-ups, I see a Rose-breasted Grosbeak framed perfectly through the skylight. Don't tell me that's not fresh-spilled blood across its breast. All morning a Blue-winged Warbler drew boundaries with its buzzy song, establishing territory. A White-eyed Vireo, a haunted bird, possessed, the work of the devil. I spend at least an hour lingering over it through the binoculars. Could not take my eyes off its white, white eyes. Why did natural selection select those white eyes?"

THE GUDASES' SPRING BACKYARD BIRD LIST
SUBURBAN   *Baton Rouge, Louisiana*

Permanent Residents. Wood Duck, Mourning Dove, Barred Owl, Red-headed Woodpecker, Red-bellied Woodpecker, Downy Woodpecker, Hairy Woodpecker, Northern Flicker, Pileated Woodpecker—NLS, Blue Jay, American Crow, Carolina Chickadee, Tufted Titmouse, Carolina Wren, Eastern Bluebird, Northern Mockingbird, Brown Thrasher, European Starling, Pine Warbler, Northern Cardinal, Rufous-sided Towhee, Chipping Sparrow, Field Sparrow, Red-winged Blackbird, Common Grackle, Brown-headed Cowbird, House Sparrow.
  Migratory Transients. Yellow Warbler, Cerulean Warbler, Black-and-white Warbler, Wilson's Warbler—Ra, Scarlet Tanager, Rose-breasted Grosbeak, Blue Grosbeak, Indigo Bunting.
  Summer Residents. Mississippi Kite, Yellow-billed Cuckoo, Chimney Swift, Ruby-throated Hummingbird, Eastern Kingbird, Blue-gray Gnatcatcher, Wood Thrush, Northern Parula, Prothonotary Warbler, Hooded Warbler, Summer Tanager, Painted Bunting, Dickcissel, Orchard Oriole, Northern Oriole.
  Winter Residents. Yellow-bellied Sapsucker, Eastern Phoebe, Ruby-crowned Kinglet, Hermit Thrush, Orange-crowned Warbler, Yellow-rumped Warbler, White-throated Sparrow.

Observations and Comments by Almena P. Gudas

"In mid-March we always put up our hummingbird feeders, and the Ruby-throats soon appear, first the males and then the females. They are with us until September or October.
  "Also in May, we hear the slightly hoarse call of the Prothonotary and soon see a flash of gold among the green of the trees. Our Orchard Orioles return about the same time.
  "Migratory birds that pass through vary from year to year. A Rose-breasted or Blue Grosbeak may stop by a feeder, a Painted Bunting may pause for a few minutes, a Northern Oriole or Scarlet Tanager may take a bath beneath the sprinkler. As any birder knows, seeing the unexpected is one of the joys of birding."

THE WILLIAMSES' SPRING BACKYARD BIRD LIST
SUBURBAN   *Silver City, New Mexico*

Permanent Residents. Northern Harrier—O, Sharp-shinned Hawk—O, Cooper's Hawk, Red-tailed Hawk, Golden Eagle—O, American Kestrel, Gambel's Quail, Killdeer—O, Mourning Dove, Greater Roadrunner, Western Screech-Owl—O, Great Horned Owl, Acorn Woodpecker, Yellow-bellied Sapsucker—O, Williamson's Sapsucker, Ladder-backed Woodpecker, Downy Woodpecker—O, Hairy Woodpecker, Northern Flicker, Say's Phoebe—O, Vermilion Flycatcher—O, Steller's Jay—O, Scrub Jay, American Crow—O, Common Raven, Plain Titmouse, Bushtit, Bewick's Wren, Western Bluebird, Townsend's Solitaire, Curve-billed Thrasher, Cedar Waxwing—O, Phainopepla—O, Loggerhead Shrike—O, Rufous-sided Towhee, Brown Towhee, House Finch.

Migratory Transients. Swainson's Hawk, Sandhill Crane—O, Lesser Nighthawk—O, Calliope Hummingbird—O, Broad-tailed Hummingbird—O, Western Wood-Peewee—O, Brown-crested Flycatcher, Solitary Vireo—O, Virginia's Warbler—O, Lucy's Warbler—O, Yellow Warbler—O, Yellow-rumped Warbler, Black-throated Gray Warbler—O, Grace's Warbler, Wilson's Warbler, Blue Grosbeak—O, Lazuli Bunting—O, Varied Bunting—Ra, Painted Bunting—Ra.

Summer Residents. Turkey Vulture, Black-chinned Hummingbird, Say's Phoebe, Ash-throated Flycatcher, Violet-green Swallow, Pinyon Jay, Northern Mockingbird, Black-headed Grosbeak.

Summer Visitors. Cassin's Kingbird, Western Kingbird, Hepatic Tanager, Rose-breasted Grosbeak—Ra, Hooded Oriole, Northern Oriole, Scott's Oriole, Pine Siskin, Lesser Goldfinch.

Observations and Comments by Harvey Williams

March.   "Mild weather but many windy days. Red-tailed Hawks incubating eggs."

April.   "Continued winds, mild temperatures, and showers. Birds that wintered here will migrate vertically to the nearby Gila Mountains: Dark-eyed Junco, Rufous-crowned Sparrow, Ruby-crowned Kinglet, Bridled Titmouse, Mountain Chickadee, Steller's Jay, White-crowned Sparrow. Northern migrating birds appear the twenty-first."

May.   "Northward migration continues with weather warm and dry. Great Horned Owls fledged."

THE KILLPACKS' SPRING BACKYARD BIRD LIST
SUBURBAN   *Ogden, Utah*

Permanent Residents. Golden Eagle—O, American Kestrel—O, Chukar—O, Northern (Red-shafted) Flicker, Scrub Jay, Black-billed Magpie, Black-capped Chickadee, Blue-gray Gnatcatcher, American Robin, Cedar Waxwing—O, European Starling, Rufous-sided Towhee, Pine Siskin—O, American Goldfinch.

Migratory Transients. Franklin's Gull—O, California Gull, Calliope Hummingbird, Rufous Hummingbird, Gray Flycatcher, Western Flycatcher, Tree Swallow, Violet-green Swallow, House Wren—O, Golden-crowned Kinglet—O, Ruby-crowned Kinglet, Swainson's Thrush, Hermit Thrush, Gray Catbird—Ra, Gray Vireo—Ra, Solitary Vireo—O, Warbling Vireo, Red-eyed Vireo—Ra, Yellow-rumped Warbler, Black-throated Gray Warbler—Ra, Kentucky Warbler—Ra, MacGillivray's Warbler, Northern Cardinal—Ra, Green-tailed Towhee, Chipping Sparrow, Song Sparrow—Ra, Lincoln's Sparrow—Ra, Cassin's Finch.

Summer Residents. Mourning Dove, Common Poorwill, Black-chinned Hummingbird, Orange-crowned Warbler, Virginia's Warbler, Yellow Warbler, Western Tanager, Black-headed Grosbeak, Lazuli Bunting, Brown-headed Cowbird, Northern Oriole.

Observations and Comments by Merlin Killpack

March.   "Warmer days, some wind and below-freezing or near-freezing weather for part and warmer by end of month. Some buds on trees and shrubs start to swell. We start to see movement in birds; new juncos show up, more robins are in evidence. Some Scrub Jays start nesting. Steller's Jay gone by end of month."

April. "Migration is evident by an occasional warbler. Lazuli Buntings by last week in April. Some sparrows, like White-crowned. Some hummingbirds migrate through into May. Black-chinned Hummingbird stays all summer and nests."

May. "Nesting birds start to arrive. The Black-headed Grosbeak by the twelfth. Lazuli Buntings reach peak of migration by the fifteenth. Warblers. Vireos. Juncos gone by end of month."

Merlin Killpack on Rare Birds

Varied Thrush.   "This is a rare bird in the state and I have banded three in fall migration and one in spring migration, which is supposed to be a first spring record for the state."

Brown Thrasher.   "Banded two in past. Very rare for state."

Northern Cardinal.   "Caught one March 15, 1983—first record for the state. When I saw it in the net I wondered who had been painting birds in the area bright red."

Lazuli Bunting.   "Years ago very rare in the area. Last three years they've numbered from 300 to over a 1000 that visit my yard and feeder. From May to June have banded large numbers—ran out of bands each year."

Howard Blume on the Rare Bird Merlin Killpack

I'm sure you won't find many, if any, Backyard Bird Lists with as many rare birds and state records as there are in Merlin's. You see, he's definitely got the advantage. It's not only that he bands birds and most of us don't. It's that he's out banding every day of the year and all day when necessary. When I talked on the phone with Merlin,

getting his recent backyard bird update, he told me that from January 1986 to October of that same year he had banded 4000 birds in his backyard. That's 4000 bands and a good deal of work, which led me to speculate on how many rare birds and records I would come up with if I gave my backyard similar attention. Merlin also told me he banded his first Kentucky Warbler that spring, which was a record not only for his backyard but for the state of Utah. That spring he also banded his first Black-throated Gray Warbler and that fall his first Townsend's Warbler, two of them, a first for the valley. But what really provoked a raising of eyebrows at the bird-banding laboratory in Laurel, Maryland, was Merlin's report of an American Redstart he banded that August. Pictures were requested of the bird—to remove any doubt. There was no doubt as far as Merlin was concerned. (He always photographs his rare birds, as a matter of course.) So off in the mail went a 35-mm slide of an American Redstart, and any doubt was put to rest.

THE MURPHYS' SPRING BACKYARD BIRD LIST
URBAN   *San Francisco, California*

Permanent Residents. California Quail—Sp, Killdeer—OV, Rock Dove, Mourning Dove, Anna's Hummingbird, American Crow—O-OV, Common Raven—OV, Chestnut-backed Chickadee, Bushtit, American Robin, Northern Mockingbird—Sp, Fa, European Starling, Brown Towhee, White-crowned Sparrow, Brewer's Blackbird, Brown-headed Cowbird, House Finch, Lesser Goldfinch, House Sparrow.
   Migratory Transients. Turkey Vulture—OV, Tree Swallow—OV.
   Summer Residents. Allen's Hummingbird.
   Winter Residents. Double-crested Cormorant—OV, Mallard—OV,

American Wigeon—OV, Mew Gull—OV, California Gull—OV, Glaucous-winged Gull—OV, Northern (Red-shafted) Flicker, Ruby-crowned Kinglet, Cedar Waxwing, Yellow-rumped Warbler, Golden-crowned Sparrow, Dark-eyed (Oregon) Junco, Pine Siskin, American Goldfinch.

Observations and Comments by Dan Murphy

March.   "Territorial behavior begins. [Remember, the nesting season begins much sooner in Dan's part of the country.] Midmonth, reduce feed by one-quarter for a week or so. Late month, reduce feed to one-half feeder capacity."

April.   "First week reduce feed to one-quarter feeder capacity. Second week stop feeding. Cedar Waxwings gather together in large flocks prior to heading north.

"We don't have a spring migration to speak of. Most of the spring migrants bypass us following the coast, San Francisco Bay, or the mountain chain to the east."

March

DATE

DATE

March

DATE _____

_____
_____
_____
_____
_____
_____
_____
_____
_____
_____
_____
_____

DATE _____

_____
_____
_____
_____
_____
_____
_____
_____
_____
_____
_____
_____

March

DATE

DATE

March

DATE

DATE

March

DATE

DATE

March

DATE _____

_____

_____

_____

_____

_____

_____

_____

_____

_____

_____

_____

_____

_____

DATE _____

_____

_____

_____

_____

_____

_____

_____

_____

_____

_____

_____

_____

_____

March

DATE

DATE

March

DATE

DATE

March

DATE

DATE

March

DATE _____

_____
_____
_____
_____
_____
_____
_____
_____
_____

DATE _____

_____
_____
_____
_____
_____
_____
_____
_____
_____

March

DATE _____

_____

_____

_____

_____

_____

_____

_____

_____

_____

_____

DATE _____

_____

_____

_____

_____

_____

_____

_____

_____

_____

_____

March

DATE

DATE

March

DATE

DATE

March

DATE _____

_____

_____

_____

_____

_____

_____

_____

_____

_____

_____

_____

DATE _____

_____

_____

_____

_____

_____

_____

_____

_____

_____

_____

_____

March

DATE _____

_____
_____
_____
_____
_____
_____
_____
_____
_____
_____
_____
_____

DATE _____

_____
_____
_____
_____
_____
_____
_____
_____
_____
_____
_____
_____

March

DATE

DATE

April

DATE _____

_____
_____
_____
_____
_____
_____
_____
_____
_____
_____
_____

DATE _____

_____
_____
_____
_____
_____
_____
_____
_____
_____
_____
_____

April

DATE

DATE

April

DATE _____

_____
_____
_____
_____
_____
_____
_____
_____
_____
_____
_____
_____

DATE _____

_____
_____
_____
_____
_____
_____
_____
_____
_____
_____
_____
_____

April

DATE

DATE

April

DATE

DATE

April

DATE

DATE

April

DATE

DATE

April

DATE

DATE

April

DATE

DATE

April

DATE

DATE

April

DATE

DATE

April

DATE _____

_____

_____

_____

_____

_____

_____

_____

_____

_____

_____

DATE _____

_____

_____

_____

_____

_____

_____

_____

_____

_____

_____

April

DATE

DATE

April

DATE _____

_____
_____
_____
_____
_____
_____
_____
_____
_____
_____
_____
_____

DATE _____

_____
_____
_____
_____
_____
_____
_____
_____
_____
_____
_____
_____

April

DATE

DATE

April

DATE

DATE

May

DATE

DATE

May

DATE

DATE

May

DATE

DATE

May

DATE _____

_____

_____

_____

_____

_____

_____

_____

_____

_____

_____

DATE _____

_____

_____

_____

_____

_____

_____

_____

_____

_____

_____

May

DATE

DATE

May

DATE

DATE

May

DATE

DATE

May

DATE

DATE

May

DATE

DATE

May

DATE

DATE

May

DATE _____

_____
_____
_____
_____
_____
_____
_____
_____
_____
_____
_____

DATE _____

_____
_____
_____
_____
_____
_____
_____
_____
_____
_____
_____

May

DATE

DATE

May

DATE _____

_____
_____
_____
_____
_____
_____
_____
_____
_____
_____
_____

DATE _____

_____
_____
_____
_____
_____
_____
_____
_____
_____
_____
_____

May

DATE _____

DATE _____

May

DATE

DATE

May

DATE _____

_____
_____
_____
_____
_____
_____
_____
_____
_____
_____
_____

DATE _____

_____
_____
_____
_____
_____
_____
_____
_____
_____
_____
_____

SUMMER

JUNE·JULY·AUGUST

THE SEVENTH of June marks the "official" end of spring migration throughout most of the country. The majority of birds will have reached their destination and have lost the urge to migrate. There are always a few stragglers that won't abide by the cutoff date and a few nonbreeding males that might stay in your backyard instead of continuing on north. Permanent and summer residents nesting in your and your neighbors' backyards will be in full song—to attract a mate and to let it be known to all of their kind that this backyard is sung for and that others should nest and forage elsewhere.

Singing gradually decreases during the month of June, but you're always guaranteed an early morning and evening chorus. There are certain birds, though, that once they've begun singing can't seem to stop—like the indefatigable Indigo Buntings that nest in most of the backyards in my neighborhood in Irvington, New York. From the beginning of June to its end the Indigo Buntings sing on unwaveringly throughout the day, sustaining top volume and expending endless amounts of vocal energy. This bird has become one of my favorite vocalists.

The Top Ten Songsters

It isn't easy narrowing a list of favorite songsters down to ten birds. Some strong contenders have to be left out. My own subjective list includes Indigo Bunting, Northern Cardinal, Northern Mockingbird, White-throated Sparrow, House Wren or Carolina Wren, Bobolink, Eastern or Western Meadowlark, Wood Thrush, Veery, and American Robin. I'll wager that no matter where in the United States you are located, all of us will at least agree upon several of the top ten.

June and July—Nesting Birds

June is the time to focus your attention on your backyard nesting birds. Some nesters will have their young out of the nest; others will still be incubating their eggs.

By July, juveniles will be in their first complete plumage, still peeping to be fed and soon trying out their wings. If you're attuned to the daily commotion of parent and young, you'll discover that at times the commotion is provoked by predators, such as your house cat, other birds, and a possible reptile or rodent. You'll soon learn to recognize a bird's alarm call.

Some species begin second broods. In my backyard in Irvington, New York, second broods seem to be trendy. The Eastern Phoebe, Gray Catbird, Northern Cardinal, House Wren, and American Robin all took on second broods for three consecutive years. Then one summer none did. Pure speculation, and I underline speculation, finds a connection between second broods and the gypsy moth explosion that purged eastern forests, woodlands, and backyards of their deciduous foliage. The first year the moths radically declined was the first year my backyard nesters ceased to raise second broods. Regular spraying of insecticides subsidized by my neighbors might have reduced not only the gypsy moth population, but also the overall insect population, leaving less food and little incentive for second broods.

Incubation, Nestlings, and Fledglings

The period of time a bird sits on its eggs keeping them warm is known as the incubation period. Several days before a bird lays its eggs, the down feathers on its belly molt, leaving a bare patch of skin that becomes heavily swollen with numerous blood vessels filled with a continuous flow of warm blood. This incubation, or brood, patch is judiciously placed over as many eggs as it can cover, each egg eventually getting its share of the warm, swollen patch. Vascularization increases throughout incubation and is sustained during the first few days of brooding for the benefit of the naked nestlings.

In some species, if both sexes incubate, both develop incubation patches. Among phalaropes, only the male incubates the eggs, and only he develops the incubation patch. Most male songbirds that share incubation with the female don't develop the patch. This fact has put some doubt on their effectiveness in incubating the eggs. However, if the male songbird isn't facilitating incubation when he sits on the eggs, at least he has provided the female with time to stretch her wings and has continued to protect the eggs.

The length of the incubation period depends on the size of the bird (larger birds have longer incubation periods) and whether the bird is altricial or precocial. Altricial young (from the Latin *altrix*, "wet nurse"), such as songbirds, are born with their eyes closed and are scrawny, usually naked, and helpless. They are completely dependent on their parents for food and care until their development is complete. Precocial young (from the Latin *praecox*, "ripened beforehand"), such as ducks and plovers, are born cute, with their eyes open and a covering of down feathers. They are able to walk or swim and feed themselves within a few hours or days after hatching.

Since precocial birds are born more fully developed than altricial birds, it follows that precocial birds' incubation periods are longer than those of similarly sized altricial birds, which must finish their development in the nest. For instance, as the accompanying table shows, the incubation period of the Killdeer, a 10½-inch precocial bird, is 24 days, whereas the incubation period of the American Robin, a 10-inch altricial bird, is only 11–14 days. The young of the

Incubation, Nestlings, and Fledglings

Altricial Birds	Incubation Days	Nestling Days
Song Sparrow (6¼″)	12–14	10
Purple Martin (8″)	15–18	26–31
American Robin (10″)	11–14	15–16
Mourning Dove (12″)	14–15	10–15

Precocial Birds	Incubation Days	Fledgling Days
Sanderling (8″)	24–31	17
Killdeer (10½″)	24	25
Common Tern (14½″)	21–26	28
Mallard (23″)	26–30	49–60

robin must then spend another 15–16 days in the nest, bringing their total development period to 26–30 days, roughly equivalent to that of the similarly sized precocial Killdeer in the egg.

Since precocial young grow to fuller development within the egg than do altricial young, it also follows that the eggs of precocial birds are larger than the eggs of similarly sized altricial birds. Also, the egg yolk—the nutritive part of the egg—is proportionately larger in the eggs of precocial birds—24%–50% of the egg's weight as opposed to 15%–25% of the egg's weight in altricial birds.

The precocial embryo needs more yolk because its incubation, and therefore its development time, is longer, because when hatched, it is going to emerge as a down-covered chick capable of seeing and soon walking, swimming, and self-feeding, whereas the altricial young, the result of a shorter incubation and less yolk, is born naked, blind, and helpless. The time an altricial young spends in the nest fed by its parents, and all the insects converted to energy by the metabolism of the altricial young, are equivalent to yolk energy and to the additional time a precocial chick has to spend in the egg. Either way, time and energy have to be invested. The results are the same—feathers and eventually flight.

Once the altricial young are hatched and ensconced in the nest, they are referred to as nestlings. From the time the altricial young leave the nest (10–30 days after hatching) until they are independent from their parents, they are referred to as fledglings. Recent altricial fledglings have flight feathers, but they're not quite sure what to do with them. They still look to their parents for sustenance, but not for long—2 to 5 days out of the nest and they're on their own.

Since precocial chicks can leave the nest soon after hatching, they do not have a nestling period and are called fledglings from the word go. Recent precocial fledglings are a long way from flying and need to rely on their parents' guidance and protection until their wings are strong and large enough to fly. The time precocial young spend as fledglings ranges from 17 to 60 days, depending on the eventual size of the young adult and the species.

The survival strategies of altricial and precocial birds are beautifully integrated with the development of the young. Altricial birds usually build well-constructed nests above ground, where the young are safe from ground-dwelling predators during their vulnerable nestling period. Precocial birds usually nest on the ground, and the ability of the young to leave the nest soon after hatching is their protection against predators.

Observing Nesting Birds

You can watch and enjoy your nesting backyard birds when the opportunity presents itself, or you can spend as much time as you can studying and recording their behavior, keeping track of their schedules, paying attention to the particulars, dealing with such events as their first arrival in your backyard, courtship, nest building, incubation, feeding of nestlings, fledglings, etc. What is the number of eggs in the clutch? What percentage of the eggs hatch? How many visits do the parents make to the nest each day to feed the young? How many days are the young blind? These are just a few questions you might ask and answer when you're observing your nesting birds.

One way to find a nest in your backyard is to stumble across it. I've never had to search for a nest. One early June morning I'd look out our bedroom window and find myself staring into the nest of an incubating robin. I inadvertently found a chickadee's nest in the hollow at the base of a tree along a path to our shed. Along that same path I visually bumped into a flicker's nest ten feet up in the hollow of a dead tree.

Another way of finding nests is to pay attention to a bird's comings and goings. During nest building, birds will be making frequent trips with nest material in their bill. During incubation, your passing by may startle a bird from its nest with a characteristic scrambling sound that is different from that of a bird taking flight from a perched position. And during the nestling period, watch for parent birds carrying insects to the nest in their bill, or carrying out little fecal sacs of the nestlings' waste material to keep the nest clean.

You can also erect birdhouses or bird shelves for your backyard birds to nest in or on. For further information, see Your Backyard as Habitat.

Whisper Songs

Primary songs are those songs birds use to attract mates and declare territory; they're the ones we are familiar with. Whisper songs are but a whisper of the primary song—a quiet inward rendition of the primary song heard no more than twenty yards away and often sung by either the male or the female while sitting on the nest. One can only guess at its purpose. Maybe like one of our lullabies, it is a means of comforting both the brooding bird who sits and sings and the life beneath. Birds who are known to sing whisper songs are the American Goldfinch, Warbling Vireo, male Gray Catbird, Rosebreasted and Black-headed Grosbeaks, and Brown Thrasher. If you spend time at the nest you might find others.

August—Postnuptial Molt and Shorebird Migration

August is usually wet and warmer than the preceding months. Some birds will be occupied with late or second broods, but August is a silent month when it comes to bird song—almost mysteriously silent, scarily silent. Many of the birds seem to have disappeared. I have to remind myself that my songless backyard is not the harbinger of Armageddon but is only due to postnuptial blues, hormones, and the loss and gain of feathers.

Because of wear and tear, birds have to replace their feathers. So they molt. Most birds molt wing and tail feathers symmetrically, one or two feathers at a time, always leaving enough feathers for flight as new ones grow in. The best time for a bird to go through its molt is when the energy demands of the breeding season are over and food is still plentiful. During this period birds become secretive and quiet, all the while fattening up and going through their molt. Every August in Irvington, New York, our neighborhood robins seem to disappear: occasionally I'll flush one or two leery ones when I take the path through our woodlot. Several weeks later they'll all reappear with a healthy new set of feathers and a renewed spirit and vitality.

Waterfowl go through postnuptial molt, except they lose their feathers all at once and become flightless. The male goes into an eclipse plumage, a dark unobtrusive garb resembling the female plumage. Both male and female go into hiding until the feathers are replaced.

August is the month for shorebirds; they are well on their way south from their northern nesting grounds. So if your backyard overlooks the beach, mud flats, or tide pools, phone me up and invite me over. I can't think of a better way to spend a day than to watch shorebirds build up their fat reserves. The fall shorebird migration is spectacular, beginning in August and lasting until late October. August is also the month of postbreeding wanderers, such as terns, gulls, and herons—birds that have a tendency to leave their original breeding grounds and wander. One year in late August, a Great Egret spent a week in a small pond adjoining our property as such a wanderer. August also brings back the swallows. Migrating swallows may fly over your backyard continuously throughout the day, and unless you look up you'll never know.

THE BLUMES' SUMMER BACKYARD BIRD LIST
SUBURBAN   *Irvington, New York*

Permanent Residents. Canada Goose—OV, Red-tailed Hawk, Ring-billed Gull—OV, Herring Gull—OV, Eastern Screech-Owl—O, Hairy Woodpecker, Pileated Woodpecker—O, Cedar Waxwing—O, American Goldfinch, House Sparrow.

Permanent Residents—Nesting. Mourning Dove, Downy Woodpecker, Blue Jay, American Crow, Black-capped Chickadee, Tufted Titmouse, White-breasted Nuthatch, Northern Mockingbird, European Starling, Northern Cardinal, Song Sparrow, House Finch.

Summer Residents. Green-backed Heron, Chimney Swift, Eastern Kingbird—O, Swainson's Thrush—O, Brown Thrasher—NLS, Yellow Warbler, Common Yellowthroat, Scarlet Tanager, Brown-headed Cowbird.

Summer Residents—Nesting. Wood Duck—Ra, Northern Flicker, Eastern Phoebe, House Wren, Veery, Gray-cheeked Thrush—O, Wood Thrush, American Robin, Gray Catbird, Red-eyed Vireo, Blue-winged Warbler, Rose-breasted Grosbeak, Indigo Bunting, Rufous-sided Towhee, Red-winged Blackbird, Common Grackle, Northern Oriole.

Summer Visitors. Turkey Vulture—OV.

Observations and Comments by Howard Blume

June 12.   "The episode smacks of Walt Disney, as if certain pages out of Peterson's *Field Guide* were suddenly thrown into animation. It took place ten feet off the path and not more than ten feet above the ground in the thick of fresh green backlit foliage. I heard a burst of short, high-pitched, frantic chirps. They belonged to a very excited Indigo Bunting that was sounding off its alarm call as it encountered a steadfast Blue Jay, whose plan was to make a meal out of the eggs in the bunting's nest. Suddenly, within seconds of the bunting's alarm call, charging out of the foliage, one appearing a second after the other, all sounding their alarm call, all ready to protect their own nest and ready to battle, were representatives of five different species. In a space of less than three cubic feet the Blue Jay was surrounded by a Blue-winged Warbler, a Red-eyed Vireo, a Gray Catbird, a House Wren, a Northern Cardinal, and the Indigo Bunting. It was too much for me and the Blue Jay to take. He flew off. I didn't believe any of it."

THE GUDASES' SUMMER BACKYARD BIRD LIST
SUBURBAN   *Baton Rouge, Louisiana*

Permanent Residents. Downy Woodpecker, Hairy Woodpecker, Northern Flicker, Pileated Woodpecker—NLS, Eastern Bluebird, Chipping Sparrow, Field Sparrow, Red-winged Blackbird.

Permanent Residents—Nesting. Wood Duck, Mourning Dove, Barred Owl, Red-headed Woodpecker, Red-bellied Woodpecker, Blue Jay, American Crow, Carolina Chickadee, Tufted Titmouse, Carolina Wren, Northern Mockingbird, Brown Thrasher, European Starling, Pine Warbler, Northern Cardinal, Rufous-sided Towhee, Common Grackle, Brown-headed Cowbird, House Sparrow.

Summer Residents. Mississippi Kite, Yellow-billed Cuckoo, Northern Parula, Hooded Warbler, Painted Bunting, Dickcissel.

Summer Residents—Nesting. Chimney Swift, Ruby-throated Hummingbird, Eastern Kingbird, Blue-gray Gnatcatcher, Wood Thrush, Prothonotary Warbler, Summer Tanager, Orchard Oriole, Northern Oriole.

Observations and Comments by Almena P. Gudas

"In late May immatures begin to appear, and we enjoy seeing young cardinals and jays fluttering their wings, begging to be fed, and later learning to come to the feeders themselves. Young cardinals continue to appear as late as September. Jays and titmouses also seem to nest more than once a year. In midsummer we see our first young woodpeckers. Also during the summer we see families of towhees, thrashers, sometimes thrushes and Orchard Orioles."

THE WILLIAMSES' SUMMER BACKYARD BIRD LIST
SUBURBAN   *Silver City, New Mexico*

Permanent Residents. Northern Harrier—O, Sharp-shinned Hawk—O, Golden Eagle—O, American Kestrel, Killdeer—O, Western Screech-Owl—O, Yellow-bellied Sapsucker—O, Williamson's Sapsucker, Downy Woodpecker—O, Hairy Woodpecker, Say's Phoebe—O, Vermilion Flycatcher—O, Steller's Jay—O, American Crow—O, Cedar Waxwing—O, Phainopepla—O, Loggerhead Shrike—O.

Permanent Residents—Nesting. Cooper's Hawk, Red-tailed Hawk, Gambel's Quail, Mourning Dove, Greater Roadrunner, Great Horned Owl, Acorn Woodpecker, Ladder-backed Woodpecker, Northern (Red-shafted) Flicker, Scrub Jay, Common Raven, Plain Titmouse, Bushtit, Bewick's Wren, Western Bluebird, Townsend's Solitaire, Curve-billed Thrasher, Rufous-sided Towhee, Brown Towhee, House Finch.

Summer Residents. Turkey Vulture.

Summer Residents—Nesting. Black-chinned Hummingbird, Say's

Phoebe, Ash-throated Flycatcher, Violet-green Swallow, Pinyon Jay, Northern Mockingbird, Black-headed Grosbeak.

Summer Visitors. Cassin's Kingbird, Western Kingbird, Hepatic Tanager, Summer Tanager, Rose-breasted Grosbeak—Ra, Hooded Oriole, Northern Oriole, Scott's Oriole, Pine Siskin, Lesser Goldfinch.

Observations and Comments by Harvey Williams

June.   "Weather hot (90°–95° F) and dry. Much nesting activity."

July.   "Summer rains start about the fourth. Daytime temps moderate to upper 80s, night temps 60°–65° F. Bird population stable. Most nestlings fledged, some birds nesting a second time. Male Rufous Hummingbirds appear."

August.   "More Rufous Hummingbirds arrive on way south. Most male Black-headed Grosbeaks leave."

THE KILLPACKS' SUMMER BACKYARD BIRD LIST
SUBURBAN   *Ogden, Utah*

Permanent Residents. Golden Eagle—O, American Kestrel—O, Chukar—O, American Robin, Cedar Waxwing—O, European Starling, Pine Siskin—O, American Goldfinch.

Permanent Residents—Nesting. Mourning Dove, Northern (Red-shafted) Flicker, Scrub Jay, Black-billed Magpie (foothills), Black-capped Chickadee, Blue-gray Gnatcatcher (foothills), Rufous-sided Towhee, House Finch.

Summer Residents. Western Tanager, Lazuli Bunting, Northern Oriole.

Summer Residents—Nesting. Mourning Dove (foothills), Common Poorwill (foothills), Black-chinned Hummingbird, Orange-crowned Warbler (foothills), Virginia's Warbler (foothills), Yellow Warbler, Black-headed Grosbeak, Brown-headed Cowbird, Northern Oriole.

Summer Visitor. American Redstart—Ra.

Observations and Comments by Merlin Killpack

July–August.   "Young of Black-headed Grosbeaks, Black-capped Chickadees, House Finches, Robins, and Scrub Jays start to appear in yard."

THE MURPHYS' SUMMER BACKYARD BIRD LIST
URBAN   *San Francisco, California*

Permanent Residents. California Quail—Sp, Killdeer—OV, Rock Dove, Anna's Hummingbird, American Crow—O-OV, Common Raven—OV, Chestnut-backed Chickadee, Bushtit, Northern Mockingbird—Sp, Fa, Brown Towhee, Brewer's Blackbird, Brown-headed Cowbird, House Finch, Lesser Goldfinch.

Permanent Residents—Nesting. Mourning Dove, American Robin, European Starling, White-crowned Sparrow, House Finch, House Sparrow.

Summer Residents. Allen's Hummingbird.

Summer Visitor. Pigmy Nuthatch.

Observations and Comments by Dan Murphy

"My backyard list is fairly representative for San Francisco. The following could also be expected in the city: Red-shouldered Hawk; Great Horned Owl; Downy Woodpecker; Violet-green, Barn, and Cliff Swallows; Varied and Hermit Thrushes; Golden-crowned Kinglet; Hutton's and Warbling Vireos; Townsend's and Wilson's Warblers; and Hooded Oriole.

"In suburban areas outside the city, oaks and conifers are more abundant, and the backyard bird life is more varied. Coastal yards will get all forms of seabirds, waterfowl, waders, and shorebirds. In addition to previously mentioned species, we can add Barn and Screech Owls; Vaux's and White-throated Swifts; Belted Kingfisher; Acorn, Hairy, and Nuttal's Woodpeckers; Red-breasted Sapsucker; Say's Phoebe; Western and Olive-sided Flycatchers; Western Wood-Pewee; Steller's Jay; Red-breasted Nuthatch; Brown Creeper; Wrentit; Winter and Bewick's Wrens; California Thrasher; Swainson's Thrush; Nashville and Black-throated Gray Warblers; Western Meadowlark; Northern Oriole; Western Tanager; Black-headed Grosbeak; Purple Finch; and Rufous-sided Towhee.

"Of course there are many more possible species. Gordon Bolander holds the record of 229 species from his yard at Bodega Bay, Sonoma County."

California, Where Records Are Made To Be Broken

California claims the highest Backyard Life Lists in the country. I expect to get several letters from other birders in other states challenging that statement, but then again, I probably won't. If you live on or near the Pacific Ocean, say at the entrance to Bolinas Lagoon, north of San Francisco, a Backyard Life List of 170 would not be unusual; Dave DeSante lives on a cliff at that entrance, and that 170 is his. Gordon Bolander, with his record of 229 (mentioned by Dan Murphy above) had a backyard of marsh and willow thickets that flooded every winter, bringing the sea closer to his front porch and also bringing in all the wintering seabirds, waterfowl, wading birds, and shorebirds; that flooding of water and birds helps explain Gordon's 229. I am told Gordon's record is already topped by another California backyard with an additional 13 birds; I have as of yet not tracked down the occupants for verification or particulars but I know they live on the coast. Also California could stand to hold the record for the Urban Backyard Life List. Mike Parmeter, who lives in Napa, California, has a Backyard Life List of 115, and he isn't even in sight of water.

June

DATE

DATE

June

DATE

DATE

June

DATE _____

_____

_____

_____

_____

_____

_____

_____

_____

_____

_____

DATE _____

_____

_____

_____

_____

_____

_____

_____

_____

_____

_____

June

DATE _____

_____

_____

_____

_____

_____

_____

_____

_____

_____

_____

_____

DATE _____

_____

_____

_____

_____

_____

_____

_____

_____

_____

_____

_____

June

DATE

DATE

June

DATE _____

_____
_____
_____
_____
_____
_____
_____
_____
_____
_____

DATE _____

_____
_____
_____
_____
_____
_____
_____
_____
_____
_____

June

DATE

DATE

June

DATE _____

_____
_____
_____
_____
_____
_____
_____
_____
_____
_____
_____

DATE _____

_____
_____
_____
_____
_____
_____
_____
_____
_____
_____
_____

June

DATE

DATE

June

DATE _____

_____

_____

_____

_____

_____

_____

_____

_____

_____

_____

DATE _____

_____

_____

_____

_____

_____

_____

_____

_____

_____

_____

June

DATE

DATE

June

DATE

DATE

June

DATE

DATE

June

DATE _____

DATE _____

June

DATE _____

_____
_____
_____
_____
_____
_____
_____
_____
_____
_____
_____
_____

DATE _____

_____
_____
_____
_____
_____
_____
_____
_____
_____
_____
_____
_____

June

DATE

DATE

July

DATE _____

_____
_____
_____
_____
_____
_____
_____
_____
_____
_____
_____

DATE _____

_____
_____
_____
_____
_____
_____
_____
_____
_____
_____
_____

July

DATE _____

_____
_____
_____
_____
_____
_____
_____
_____
_____
_____

DATE _____

_____
_____
_____
_____
_____
_____
_____
_____
_____
_____

July

DATE

DATE

July

DATE _____

_____

_____

_____

_____

_____

_____

_____

_____

_____

_____

DATE _____

_____

_____

_____

_____

_____

_____

_____

_____

_____

_____

July

DATE

DATE

July

DATE _____

DATE _____

July

DATE _____

_____
_____
_____
_____
_____
_____
_____
_____
_____
_____
_____
_____

DATE _____

_____
_____
_____
_____
_____
_____
_____
_____
_____
_____
_____
_____

July

DATE _____

_____

_____

_____

_____

_____

_____

_____

_____

_____

_____

DATE _____

_____

_____

_____

_____

_____

_____

_____

_____

_____

_____

July

DATE

DATE

July

DATE _____

_____
_____
_____
_____
_____
_____
_____
_____
_____
_____
_____

DATE _____

_____
_____
_____
_____
_____
_____
_____
_____
_____
_____
_____

July

DATE _____

DATE _____

July

DATE

DATE

July

DATE

DATE

July

DATE _____

DATE _____

_____

_____

_____

_____

_____

_____

_____

_____

_____

_____

_____

_____

July

DATE

DATE

July

DATE _____

_____
_____
_____
_____
_____
_____
_____
_____
_____
_____
_____
_____
_____
_____

DATE _____

_____
_____
_____
_____
_____
_____
_____
_____
_____
_____
_____
_____
_____
_____

August

DATE

DATE

August

DATE _____

_____
_____
_____
_____
_____
_____
_____
_____
_____
_____
_____

DATE _____

_____
_____
_____
_____
_____
_____
_____
_____
_____
_____
_____

August

DATE _____

_____

_____

_____

_____

_____

_____

_____

_____

_____

_____

DATE _____

_____

_____

_____

_____

_____

_____

_____

_____

_____

_____

August

DATE

DATE

August

DATE

DATE

August

DATE _____

_____
_____
_____
_____
_____
_____
_____
_____
_____
_____

DATE _____

_____
_____
_____
_____
_____
_____
_____
_____
_____
_____

August

DATE

DATE

August

DATE _____

_____
_____
_____
_____
_____
_____
_____
_____
_____
_____
_____
_____
_____

DATE _____

_____
_____
_____
_____
_____
_____
_____
_____
_____
_____
_____
_____
_____

August

DATE _____

_____

_____

_____

_____

_____

_____

_____

_____

_____

DATE _____

_____

_____

_____

_____

_____

_____

_____

_____

_____

August

DATE _____

_____
_____
_____
_____
_____
_____
_____
_____
_____
_____
_____

DATE _____

_____
_____
_____
_____
_____
_____
_____
_____
_____
_____
_____

August

DATE

DATE

August

DATE

DATE

August

DATE

DATE

August

DATE _____

_____

_____

_____

_____

_____

_____

_____

_____

_____

DATE _____

_____

_____

_____

_____

_____

_____

_____

_____

_____

August

DATE _____

_____

_____

_____

_____

_____

_____

_____

_____

_____

_____

_____

DATE _____

_____

_____

_____

_____

_____

_____

_____

_____

_____

_____

_____

August

DATE _____

_____

_____

_____

_____

_____

_____

_____

_____

_____

_____

_____

DATE _____

_____

_____

_____

_____

_____

_____

_____

_____

_____

_____

_____

FALL

SEPTEMBER·OCTOBER·NOVEMBER

TWICE A YEAR comes the event—migration. After spring migration to its nesting ground a bird has approximately three months to mate, incubate eggs, fledge young, recuperate and fatten up, molt, and then maybe find a few weeks' breather before it is time for fall migration, this time to the south, where winter food supplies will be more abundant than in colder northern climes. Blackpoll Warblers that breed in our northern forests migrate every fall to the Atlantic Coast. Their destination is Central and South America. The Blackpolls and other songbirds, once situated at the coast, have two choices. Some will follow the coastline to South America, whereas others will take off over the Atlantic and fly 2300 nonstop miles, eighty-six nonstop hours, approaching an altitude of 21,000 oxygen-starved feet. Give that some thought when you see a half-ounce fall migrant refueling in your backyard. By September most landbirds and early waterfowl are on their way south from their northern nesting grounds to their winter homes. Remember, your backyard could be their winter home. From September through November, your winter residents will be arriving. Greet them, and hungry migrants, with a well-stocked feeder. September 15 is the average date for the maximum numbers of species coming through, but the fall migration continues on until late November and can be unpredictable.

Confusing fall warblers will be coming through in various stages of their winter plumage, some looking quite different from the way you saw them in spring. Identifying them requires a more attentive study of your field guide, greater concentration when looking through your binoculars, and several years of experience. Some of us let them pass as confusing fall warblers. Others rise to the challenge.

It's time to pay attention to the weather again. Keep in touch with cool fronts and northeast winds; they'll be carrying flycatchers, vireos, warblers, blackbirds, and sparrows. If you're on the beach and it's the month of September, you are in for it—shorebirds, gulls, and terns will be bountiful. Swallows will be filling the skys, fields, and beaches or any open area.

Fall Flocking

Sometime in September, certain species of birds that normally keep to themselves throughout the nesting season gather together in small or large flocks. One comes to look forward to these fall flockings. Like the color change of the leaves, they mark the advent of fall and the closeness of winter, and they ignite an uneasiness in me that isn't put to rest until I lower the storm windows and split wood. I've got their message.

Throughout September and October you'll see the creation of these flocks in the sky above your backyard. Back and forth and back and forth they fly, here and there, there and here, daily increasing in their numbers until one September day, streams of birds will fly over your backyard for forty minutes at a time, and just when you think the sky has finally cleared of them and you're sure that's the end of it, you'll see a few stragglers that are really the vanguard of another forty minutes of birds. And then, just to make life more interesting, they'll begin to head back in the direction they came from.

One of these fall flockers is the Common Grackle, a sleek, sensual, and glistening black bird with an iridescent purple head, a bronze purple back, white eyes, and a distinctive, long, keel-shaped tail. Flocks of grackles roost in the trees in my backyard in Irvington, New York, in the fall. First I'll hear their rusty, hoarse creakings, and then I'll gradually discover them, a hundred or more, hidden in the dense foliage.

One day in November the grackles will make their final pass over my backyard and head south, not too far south, maybe to Kentucky or Arkansas, where they'll join other grackles and blackbirds to set up their winter roosts—roosts of hundreds, thousands, and, I am told, millions. A roost is a place, such as a group of trees or shrubs, where flocks of birds gather to retire for the evening. If you happen to live near a roost, you'll have the opportunity of watching a thousand black birds darken the sky as they fly back and forth from roost to foraging grounds. It's an impressive daily event unless you live too close to the roost. Then you'll have no choice but to retain a roost buster, who through annoyance devices will convince the grackles and blackbirds to roost elsewhere. The results of a thousand birds digesting a day's worth of forage in your backyard is too much for anyone to handle.

Blue Jays flock in the fall. Their flocks aren't as large as grackles' (15 to 40), but you won't miss them flying over your backyard or sounding off in it. Blue Jay flocks have a reputation for being noisy, and they have a vocal repertoire to back it up: they've got their typical jay cry, they've got a high-pitched shriek when an enemy is discovered, they can make a very effective bell-like sound, and they can imitate a number of bird calls, such as the plaintive cry of our resident Red-tailed Hawk. I always feel "had" when I am stirred by a Redtail's call only to look up and find an empty sky and seconds later a Blue Jay. Don't get me wrong—I'm not complaining. Blue Jay flocks have become one of my September-through-February expectations. Other birds that flock in the fall are Pinyon Jays, Scrub Jays, European Starlings, Red-winged Blackbirds, and American Robins.

September Nighthawks

They're not hawks. They're not strictly nocturnal. They're essence of hawk. Their wings are long and pointed, shaped like a boomerang, and their body is built like a bullet. They have an enormous mouth, capable of opening as wide as their head. If you have never seen a Common Nighthawk before, look one up in your field guide.

When I was growing up in Chicago, Common Nighthawks were part of my midwest urban experience. Flat, graveled rooftops suffice for a nighthawk's nesting site as much as open fields, beaches, and burnt-over forests do. All summer, from the warm glow of early evening sunlight on into the varying densities of nightfall, one could watch their erratic, darting, swift silhouettes, hundreds of them gleaning insects from Chicago's skyline, from the glow of streetlamps, from above and in between apartment buildings, and from the air space above city parks and the lakefront. At night in a church parking lot I'd hear their short, emphatic, constant buzzlike screams while necking with my girl in the front seat of my father's Chevy.

After I left Chicago, six years went by without a nighthawk crossing my mind. Then one warm September day I happened to look up from my backyard in Irvington, New York, to see the sky crowded with migrating nighthawks feeding on the wing. Since then, every first or second week in September when I am in my backyard working, an inner clock goes off, telling me it's time to look up. Out of seven Septembers of looking up, expecting to see migrating nighthawks, I have been rewarded four times. Now I might be unconsciously prompted by the nighthawks' calling, but when I look up and see them it doesn't feel like that's what happened. To me it feels spontaneous, mystical, satisfying, a tenuous rendezvous kept every September a hundred feet in the air over my backyard. Check it out for yourself. Common Nighthawks are found throughout most of the United States.

Following are sample reports of the Common Nighthawk migration excerpted from the March-April 1984 issue of *American Birds*, reporting the regional findings of the 1983 fall migration throughout the United States:

Northeastern Maritime Region. It was an exceptionally good year for Com. Nighthawks migrating through the Connecticut River Valley in w. Massachusetts. In Southwick, Mass., 5169 were observed Aug. 20–Sept. 4, with a peak of 2756 Aug. 28.

Southern Atlantic Coast Region. Several thousand Com. Nighthawks—an excellent flight near Atlanta Sept. 3, and very late birds in North Carolina in New Bern Nov. 1 and Fayetteville Nov. 6.

Western Great Lake Region. Thousands of Com. Nighthawks were observed migrating along L. Superior at Silver Bay Aug. 25. Two days later in Wisconsin 1500 seen passing over Richland and 3300 over Norwalk.

Prairie Province Region. A very late Com. Nighthawk migration was reported in s. Manitoba where 146 were seen at Winnipeg Sept. 25.

Southern Great Plains. A late Com. Nighthawk lingered in Johnston, Kans., until Oct. 29. A flock of Com. Nighthawks comprising 120 birds swept across Washington, Okla., Sept. 15.

Southern Texas Region. Com. Nighthawks moved through the Austin area in impressive numbers in late August. Several hundred foraged in the bright lights of the state's capitol dome on the night of Aug. 28. As many as six were still being seen there on the very late date of Nov. 15.

October Migrations

October sees the tail end of the songbird migrants—late thrushes, warblers, and sparrows. Waterfowl will be coming through, reaching the maximum numbers by November. Hawk migration is evident in September and peaks in October. If you're along the shore, any shore, there is the possibility of Osprey, Northern Harriers, and Peregrine Falcons. And no matter where your backyard is, don't write off the possibility of sampling the hawk migration. You and your backyard have to be in the right place at the right time, but the right place doesn't have to be Pennsylvania's Hawk Mountain, a well-known migratory route for hawks. Try to be out in your backyard on a windy day following a cold front. In my backyard in Irvington, New York, when the timing and weather are right, I'll witness a decent run of Broad-winged Hawks drifting over throughout the day. I'm not sure if this backyard is on any particular migration route for Broadwings: I haven't seen them every year, but that doesn't mean they didn't fly over. It comes down to the weather, my schedule, their schedule, and serendipity. Sharp-shinned Hawks always pass by from September to November. Often they'll stay around our backyard for several days, taking advantage of the birds at the feeder.

A Fall Alert

Many of the fall migrants that pass through our backyards winter in the tropical forests of southern Mexico, Central America, the Caribbean, and South America. There is recent concern that in the foreseeable future, much of the tropical forests won't be standing when the migrants return. Farming, ranching, logging, mining, and roads are consuming forest and permanently altering habitat at the rate of twenty-five to fifty acres a minute, which computes to almost total deforestation by the end of the century—if we are to believe the worst and the experts.

This much we unfortunately do know—the tropical forest throughout the world has been decimated and continues to be. With it goes an enormous variety of one-of-a-kind plant and animal life and the winter grounds of many of our songbirds.

Reports begin to filter in from isolated researchers working in the field—the songbird population shows signs of decline. Several of the birds they are concerned with are the Kentucky Warbler, Red-eyed Vireo, American Redstart, and Ovenbird. These birds are not breeding in the habitat and range they are usually found in. No one as yet knows for sure why. Speculation has it that habitat alteration and loss in the United States could be part of the problem, but as of date, not enough fieldwork has been put in or data collected to be conclusive. The problem can also stem from loss of migrants' winter habitat in the Caribbean and Central and South America. The Bachman's Warbler, on the endangered species list, nearly extinct or possibly extinct, is a likely example of the latter. The warbler's wintering grounds in Cuba and surrounding islands are now largely sugarcane fields.

We will have to wait for further word from our professionals in the field to know how serious the problem is or will be; to know if we are witnessing normal fluctuations in population and breeding range, or if indeed there is a downward trend. As an individual birder, it isn't easy or sensible to assess the health of the songbird population from one's backyard experience. But once informed of the possible danger, it's difficult to remain unbiased, unemotional, or uninvolved. For four years I did not see one Nashville Warbler in my backyard: certainly not an indication of declining Nashvilles. Then one spring day in my yard, a single red maple tree held over a hundred Nashville Warblers: certainly not a definitive indicator of a healthy Nashville population, but a good and comforting sign.

Given the awareness of a declining songbird population, I now find myself approaching fall migration with the same zeal and attention I give to spring migration. I now count the number of Redstarts that come through my backyard or, for that matter, any migrants that winter in Latin America or the West Indies. When I see a Bay-breasted Warbler I think Panama, Venezuela; when I see a Blackburnian Warbler—Costa Rica, Peru; Hermit Thrush—Guatemala; Red-eyed Vireo—Amazon Basin; Scarlet Tanager—Columbia, Amazonia. I now find myself paying a little more attention to the politics of the Latin American countries, and I am anxious to hear about the efforts of groups like the Nature Conservancy, the World Wildlife Fund, and the Sierra Club, which are attempting to negotiate the protection of the tropical forest. The reports from the field tell us that Red-eyed Vireos aren't nesting in small woodlots as much as they have, but they are nesting in my small woodlot and have been for seven years. So now each spring I wait for the Red-eyes to return and then follow them through their breeding cycle. I want to keep track. I want to keep in touch. I want to see if my backyard migrants and summer nesters reflect the loss indicated by these recent findings. Your backyard lists, observations, and data, carefully and regularly kept, can be part of the answer researchers are looking for.

Sixteen Birds Most Likely to Succeed

Let's take a look at our five backyards and make another list, a list of birds they all have in common. Since each backyard differs in climate and terrain, the birds that make up this common list would not be considered specialists, confined to a limited habitat and limited

Sixteen Birds Most Likely to Succeed

	WILLIAMSES Silver City, NM Suburban	GUDASES Baton Rouge, LA Suburban	BLUMES Irvington, NY Suburban	KILLPACKS Ogden, UT Surburban	MURPHYS San Francisco, CA Urban
Mourning Dove	PR-N	PR-N	PR-N	SR-N	PR-N
Downy Woodpecker	PR-O	PR-N	PR-N	WR	
Northern Flicker	PR	PR-N	SR-N	PR-N	WR
American Crow	PR	PR	PR-N		PR-O
Ruby-crowned Kinglet	WV	WR	MT	WR	WR
American Robin	WV	WV	SR-N	PR-N	PR-N
Northern Mockingbird	SR-N	PR-N	PR-N		PR-O
Cedar Waxwing	PR-O	WV	PR-O	PR-O	WR
European Starling		PR-N	PR-N	PR-N	PR-N
Yellow-winged Warbler	MT	WR	MT	MT	WR
Rufous-sided Towhee	PR-N	PR-W	SR-N	PR	
Dark-eyed Junco	WR		WR	WR	WR
Brown-headed Cowbird		PR-N	SR	SR-N	PR
House Finch	PR-N	PR-N	PR-N		PR-N
Pine Siskin	SV	WV	PR-O	PR-O	WR-O
American Goldfinch		WV	PR	PR-O	WR

food source. Their specialty is not having a specialty. They can compromise; they can adjust and take advantage of a number of conditions, natural or manmade—especially manmade. The common denominator among these birds is human residences, backyards—which tells us about their adaptability and, if given some thought, about what they can do for our adaptability. When we must move—as so often we do these days—from one part of the country to another, leaving behind a history of friends, places, and events, we'll find some consolation and continuity in the sight of a familiar bird perched in our newly acquired backyard. Mourning Dove, Northern Flicker, Ruby-crowned Kinglet, American Robin, Cedar Waxwing, Yellow-rumped Warbler, and Pine Siskin are found in all of the five backyards. American Crow, Downy Woodpecker, Northern Mockingbird, Brown-headed Cowbird, European Starling, House Finch, American Goldfinch, Rufous-sided Towhee, and Dark-eyed Junco are found in all but one. I have a feeling that most of us won't appreciate any continuity a starling might bring, but there is something to be said about the bird's ability to adapt and survive.

THE BLUMES' FALL BACKYARD BIRD LIST
SUBURBAN   *Irvington, New York*

Permanent Residents. Canada Goose—OV, Red-tailed Hawk, Ring-billed Gull—OV, Herring Gull—OV, Mourning Dove, Eastern Screech-Owl—O, Downy Woodpecker, Hairy Woodpecker, Pileated Woodpecker—O, Blue Jay, American Crow, Black-capped Chickadee, Tufted Titmouse, White-breasted Nuthatch, Northern Mockingbird, Cedar Waxwing—O, European Starling, Northern Cardinal, Song Sparrow, House Finch, American Goldfinch, House Sparrow.

Migratory Transients. Great Blue Heron, Great Egret—Ra, Sharp-shinned Hawk, Broad-winged Hawk, Common Nighthawk, Tree Swallow, Barn Swallow, Carolina Wren, Winter Wren, Golden-crowned Kinglet, Ruby-crowned Kinglet, Black-throated Blue Warbler, Yellow-rumped Warbler, Black-throated Green Warbler, Black-and-white Warbler, Fox Sparrow.

Winter Residents. American Tree Sparrow—O, White-throated Sparrow, Dark-eyed (Slate-colored) Junco, Pine Siskin—O.

Observations and Comments by Howard Blume

October 26, 1980.   "Before I fill the feeders I wait for the trees to shed their last few leaves, for the cold to take its daily hold, and for the last of the sharpies to migrate through. The feeders've hung empty since last April, and that's usually my plan, to fill them when all the conditions are met. That was my plan for the last five years and that was my plan for this year—until today. Near the back entrance to our house hang two empty feeders, and on the deck nearby stands a garbage can freshly filled with bird seed. As I walked up the path toward the rear of the house I noticed a Black-capped Chickadee flitting back and forth from the garbage can lid to the empty feeder. When I came closer the chickadee accelerated and burst into song. I stood five feet away, between the feeder and the garbage can; the chickadee zipped back and forth from one to the other, while sounding off an excited, loud, rapid series of *chick-a-dee-dee-dees*. Is that chickadee trying to tell me something? Could he be telling me it's time. 'Winter is here—to hell with your plan. Let's get on with it.' I got on with it. I filled the feeder. Silence once again, and I could hear the flutter of his wings as he flew to the feeder; he picked himself a sunflower seed. Is this Black-capped Chickadee's behavior the result of seeing me lift that garbage can lid for the past five winters, scoop up a plastic pitcher full of bird seed and pour it into the feeder? Can a Black-capped Chickadee develop expectations? Make demands?"

THE GUDASES' FALL BACKYARD BIRD LIST
SUBURBAN   *Baton Rouge, Louisiana*

Permanent Residents. Wood Duck, Mourning Dove, Barred Owl, Red-headed Woodpecker, Red-bellied Woodpecker, Downy Woodpecker, Hairy Woodpecker, Northern Flicker, Pileated Woodpecker—NLS, Blue Jay, American Crow, Carolina Chickadee, Tufted Titmouse, Carolina Wren, Eastern Bluebird, Northern Mockingbird, Brown Thrasher, European Starling, Pine Warbler, Northern Cardinal, Rufous-sided Towhee, Chipping Sparrow, Field Sparrow, Red-winged Blackbird, Common Grackle, Brown-headed Cowbird, House Sparrow.

Migratory Transients. Western Kingbird, Veery, Yellow Warbler, Cerulean Warbler, Blue Grosbeak.

Winter Residents. Yellow-bellied Sapsucker, Eastern Phoebe, Ruby-crowned Kinglet, Hermit Thrush, Orange-crowned Warbler, Yellow-rumped Warbler, White-throated Sparrow.

Observations and Comments by Almena P. Gudas

"In the fall we look forward to visitors that stay all winter or stop by for a few days or weeks. We can always count on a flock of White-throated Sparrows that hop and scratch about the yard. They usually come in November and remain until spring."

The Williamses' Fall Backyard Bird List
SUBURBAN   *Silver City, New Mexico*

Permanent Residents. Northern Harrier—O, Sharp-shinned Hawk—O, Cooper's Hawk, Red-tailed Hawk, Golden Eagle—O, American Kestrel, Gambel's Quail, Killdeer—O, Mourning Dove, Greater Roadrunner, Western Screech-Owl—O, Great Horned Owl, Acorn Woodpecker, Yellow-bellied Sapsucker—O, Williamson's Sapsucker, Ladder-backed Woodpecker, Downy Woodpecker—O, Hairy Woodpecker, Northern Flicker, Say's Phoebe—O, Vermilion Flycatcher—O, Steller's Jay—O, Scrub Jay, American Crow—O, Common Raven, Plain Titmouse, Bushtit, Bewick's Wren, Western Bluebird, Townsend's Solitaire, Curve-billed Thrasher, Cedar Waxwing—O, Phainopepla—O, Loggerhead Shrike—O, Rufous-sided Towhee, Brown Towhee, House Finch.

Migratory Transients. Swainson's Hawk, Rufous Hummingbird, Virginia's Warbler, Lucy's Warbler, Yellow Warbler, Chipping Sparrow.

Winter Residents. White-breasted Nuthatch, White-crowned Sparrow, Dark-eyed (Oregon, Gray-headed) Junco.

Observations and Comments by Harvey Williams

September.   "Weather similar to August, but with declining day and night temperatures. Various species of southward migrating birds are briefly sighted."

October.   "Rains are tapering off. Temperatures noticeably cooler. Most nonresidents have left. Northern raptors arrive at month's end."

November.   "Dry, pleasant weather. Many sunny days. Winter residents arriving from mountains to the north."

The Killpacks' Fall Backyard Bird List
SUBURBAN   *Ogden, Utah*

Permanent Residents. Golden Eagle—O, American Kestrel—O, Chukar—O, Northern (Red-shafted) Flicker, Scrub Jay, Black-billed Magpie, Black-capped Chickadee, Blue-gray Gnatcatcher, American Robin, Cedar Waxwing—O, European Starling, Rufous-sided Towhee, Pine Siskin—O, American Goldfinch.

Migratory Transients. Northern Pygmy-Owl—Ra, Calliope Hummingbird, Rufous Hummingbird, Gray Flycatcher, Western Flycatcher, Tree Swallow, Violet-green Swallow, Brown Thrasher—Ra, Loggerhead Shrike—Ra, Brown Creeper—Ra, House Wren—O, Varied Thrush—Ra, Hermit Thrush, Warbling Vireo, Townsend's Warbler, Ovenbird—Ra, MacGillivray's Warbler, Wilson's Warbler, Green-tailed Towhee, Lincoln's Sparrow—Ra.

Winter Residents. Sharp-shinned Hawk, Downy Woodpecker, Mountain Chickadee, Ruby-crowned Kinglet, Townsend's Solitaire, Bohemian Waxwing, White-crowned Sparrow, Dark-eyed (Slate-colored—O, Pink-sided, Gray-headed) Junco.

Observations and Comments by Merlin Killpack

September.   "Starting to get fall rain. Hummingbirds leave by the fifteenth. You can see other birds gathering in flocks, like robins, swallows, etc., getting ready for migration. Some leaves on maple, sumacs, etc., starting to turn color. Some warblers migrating through."

October.   "Snow starts in mountains. Leaves start turning color and some fallen by middle October. Juncos start migrating back south by middle and last week. Most come in November. By November most all migrating birds have left or passed through—we get some stragglers into December, depending on the weather."

THE MURPHYS' FALL BACKYARD BIRD LIST

URBAN   *San Francisco, California*

Permanent Residents. California Quail—Sp, Killdeer—OV, Rock Dove, Mourning Dove, Anna's Hummingbird, American Crow—O-OV, Common Raven—OV, Chestnut-backed Chickadee, Bushtit, American Robin, Northern Mockingbird—Sp, Fa, European Starling, Brown Towhee, White-crowned Sparrow, Brewer's Blackbird, Brown-headed Cowbird, House Finch, Lesser Goldfinch, House Sparrow.

Migratory Transients. Red-tailed Hawk—OV, Caspian Tern—OV, Orange-crowned Warbler, Fox Sparrow, Song Sparrow—Ra.

Winter Residents. Double-crested Cormorant—OV, Mallard—OV, American Wigeon—OV, Mew Gull—OV, California Gull—OV, Glaucous-winged Gull—OV, Northern (Red-shafted) Flicker, Ruby-crowned Kinglet, Cedar Waxwing, Yellow-rumped Warbler, Golden-crowned Sparrow, Dark-eyed (Oregon) Junco, Pine Siskin, American Goldfinch.

Observations and Comments by Dan Murphy

"Our fall migration is a bit more prolific than spring, probably because of the dispersal activities of young birds." [Young birds have a tendency to leave their original home sites and explore new territory.]

October.   "Start feeding by second week."

September

DATE

DATE

September

DATE _____

_____
_____
_____
_____
_____
_____
_____
_____
_____
_____

DATE _____

_____
_____
_____
_____
_____
_____
_____
_____
_____
_____

September

DATE

DATE

September

DATE _____

_____

_____

_____

_____

_____

_____

_____

_____

_____

_____

_____

DATE _____

_____

_____

_____

_____

_____

_____

_____

_____

_____

_____

_____

September

DATE

DATE

September

DATE _____

_____

_____

_____

_____

_____

_____

_____

_____

_____

_____

_____

DATE _____

_____

_____

_____

_____

_____

_____

_____

_____

_____

_____

_____

September

DATE _____

_____
_____
_____
_____
_____
_____
_____
_____
_____
_____
_____
_____

DATE _____

_____
_____
_____
_____
_____
_____
_____
_____
_____
_____
_____
_____

September

DATE

DATE

September

DATE _____

_____

_____

_____

_____

_____

_____

_____

_____

_____

_____

DATE _____

_____

_____

_____

_____

_____

_____

_____

_____

_____

_____

September

DATE

DATE

September

DATE

DATE

September

DATE

DATE

September

DATE _____

_____

_____

_____

_____

_____

_____

_____

_____

_____

_____

DATE _____

_____

_____

_____

_____

_____

_____

_____

_____

_____

_____

_____

September

DATE _____

_____

_____

_____

_____

_____

_____

_____

_____

_____

_____

DATE _____

_____

_____

_____

_____

_____

_____

_____

_____

_____

_____

September

DATE

DATE

September

DATE _____

_____
_____
_____
_____
_____
_____
_____
_____
_____
_____

DATE _____

_____
_____
_____
_____
_____
_____
_____
_____
_____
_____

October

DATE

DATE

October

DATE

DATE

October

DATE _____

_____

_____

_____

_____

_____

_____

_____

_____

_____

_____

_____

DATE _____

_____

_____

_____

_____

_____

_____

_____

_____

_____

_____

_____

October

DATE _____

_____

_____

_____

_____

_____

_____

_____

_____

_____

_____

DATE _____

_____

_____

_____

_____

_____

_____

_____

_____

_____

_____

October

DATE

DATE

October

DATE

DATE

October

DATE

DATE

October

DATE _____

_____
_____
_____
_____
_____
_____
_____
_____
_____
_____
_____

DATE _____

_____
_____
_____
_____
_____
_____
_____
_____
_____
_____
_____

October

DATE

DATE

October

DATE _____

_____

_____

_____

_____

_____

_____

_____

_____

_____

_____

_____

DATE _____

_____

_____

_____

_____

_____

_____

_____

_____

_____

_____

_____

October

DATE _____

_____

_____

_____

_____

_____

_____

_____

_____

_____

_____

_____

DATE _____

_____

_____

_____

_____

_____

_____

_____

_____

_____

_____

_____

October

DATE

DATE

October

DATE

DATE

October

DATE

DATE

October

DATE

DATE

October

DATE _____

_____

_____

_____

_____

_____

_____

_____

_____

_____

_____

_____

DATE _____

_____

_____

_____

_____

_____

_____

_____

_____

_____

_____

_____

November

DATE

DATE

November

DATE

DATE

November

DATE

DATE

November

DATE

DATE

November

DATE

DATE

November

DATE

DATE

November

DATE _____

_____
_____
_____
_____
_____
_____
_____
_____
_____
_____
_____
_____
_____
_____

DATE _____

_____
_____
_____
_____
_____
_____
_____
_____
_____
_____
_____
_____
_____
_____

November

DATE

DATE

November

DATE

DATE

November

DATE

DATE

November

DATE

DATE

November

DATE _____

_____

_____

_____

_____

_____

_____

_____

_____

_____

_____

_____

DATE _____

_____

_____

_____

_____

_____

_____

_____

_____

_____

_____

_____

November

DATE

DATE

November

DATE

DATE

November

DATE

DATE

November

DATE

DATE

Backyard Life List

1	DATE		16	DATE
2	DATE		17	DATE
3	DATE		18	DATE
4	DATE		19	DATE
5	DATE		20	DATE
6	DATE		21	DATE
7	DATE		22	DATE
8	DATE		23	DATE
9	DATE		24	DATE
10	DATE		25	DATE
11	DATE		26	DATE
12	DATE		27	DATE
13	DATE		28	DATE
14	DATE		29	DATE
15	DATE		30	DATE

Backyard Life List

31	DATE	46	DATE
32	DATE	47	DATE
33	DATE	48	DATE
34	DATE	49	DATE
35	DATE	50	DATE
36	DATE	51	DATE
37	DATE	52	DATE
38	DATE	53	DATE
39	DATE	54	DATE
40	DATE	55	DATE
41	DATE	56	DATE
42	DATE	57	DATE
43	DATE	58	DATE
44	DATE	59	DATE
45	DATE	60	DATE

Backyard Life List

61 _____ DATE _____	76 _____ DATE _____
62 _____ DATE _____	77 _____ DATE _____
63 _____ DATE _____	78 _____ DATE _____
64 _____ DATE _____	79 _____ DATE _____
65 _____ DATE _____	80 _____ DATE _____
66 _____ DATE _____	81 _____ DATE _____
67 _____ DATE _____	82 _____ DATE _____
68 _____ DATE _____	83 _____ DATE _____
69 _____ DATE _____	84 _____ DATE _____
70 _____ DATE _____	85 _____ DATE _____
71 _____ DATE _____	86 _____ DATE _____
72 _____ DATE _____	87 _____ DATE _____
73 _____ DATE _____	88 _____ DATE _____
74 _____ DATE _____	89 _____ DATE _____
75 _____ DATE _____	90 _____ DATE _____

Backyard Life List

91	DATE		106	DATE
92	DATE		107	DATE
93	DATE		108	DATE
94	DATE		109	DATE
95	DATE		110	DATE
96	DATE		111	DATE
97	DATE		112	DATE
98	DATE		113	DATE
99	DATE		114	DATE
100	DATE		115	DATE
101	DATE		116	DATE
102	DATE		117	DATE
103	DATE		118	DATE
104	DATE		119	DATE
105	DATE		120	DATE

Backyard Life List

121	DATE	136	DATE
122	DATE	137	DATE
123	DATE	138	DATE
124	DATE	139	DATE
125	DATE	140	DATE
126	DATE	141	DATE
127	DATE	142	DATE
128	DATE	143	DATE
129	DATE	144	DATE
130	DATE	145	DATE
131	DATE	146	DATE
132	DATE	147	DATE
133	DATE	148	DATE
134	DATE	149	DATE
135	DATE	150	DATE

Backyard Life List

151	DATE	166	DATE
152	DATE	167	DATE
153	DATE	168	DATE
154	DATE	169	DATE
155	DATE	170	DATE
156	DATE	171	DATE
157	DATE	172	DATE
158	DATE	173	DATE
159	DATE	174	DATE
160	DATE	175	DATE
161	DATE	176	DATE
162	DATE	177	DATE
163	DATE	178	DATE
164	DATE	179	DATE
165	DATE	180	DATE

Backyard Life List

181	DATE	196	DATE
182	DATE	197	DATE
183	DATE	198	DATE
184	DATE	199	DATE
185	DATE	200	DATE
186	DATE	201	DATE
187	DATE	202	DATE
188	DATE	203	DATE
189	DATE	204	DATE
190	DATE	205	DATE
191	DATE	206	DATE
192	DATE	207	DATE
193	DATE	208	DATE
194	DATE	209	DATE
195	DATE	210	DATE

Backyard Life List

211	DATE
212	DATE
213	DATE
214	DATE
215	DATE
216	DATE
217	DATE
218	DATE
219	DATE
220	DATE
221	DATE
222	DATE
223	DATE
224	DATE
225	DATE

226	DATE
227	DATE
228	DATE
229	DATE
230	DATE
231	DATE
232	DATE
233	DATE
234	DATE
235	DATE
236	DATE
237	DATE
238	DATE
239	DATE
240	DATE

Backyard Big Year

DATE	TOTAL	DATE	TOTAL
DATE	TOTAL	DATE	TOTAL
DATE	TOTAL	DATE	TOTAL
DATE	TOTAL	DATE	TOTAL
DATE	TOTAL	DATE	TOTAL
DATE	TOTAL	DATE	TOTAL
DATE	TOTAL	DATE	TOTAL
DATE	TOTAL	DATE	TOTAL
DATE	TOTAL	DATE	TOTAL
DATE	TOTAL	DATE	TOTAL
DATE	TOTAL	DATE	TOTAL
DATE	TOTAL	DATE	TOTAL
DATE	TOTAL	DATE	TOTAL
DATE	TOTAL	DATE	TOTAL

Backyard Big Year

DATE	TOTAL	DATE	TOTAL
DATE	TOTAL	DATE	TOTAL
DATE	TOTAL	DATE	TOTAL
DATE	TOTAL	DATE	TOTAL
DATE	TOTAL	DATE	TOTAL
DATE	TOTAL	DATE	TOTAL
DATE	TOTAL	DATE	TOTAL
DATE	TOTAL	DATE	TOTAL
DATE	TOTAL	DATE	TOTAL
DATE	TOTAL	DATE	TOTAL
DATE	TOTAL	DATE	TOTAL
DATE	TOTAL	DATE	TOTAL
DATE	TOTAL	DATE	TOTAL
DATE	TOTAL	DATE	TOTAL
DATE	TOTAL	DATE	TOTAL

Backyard Big Year

DATE	TOTAL	DATE	TOTAL
DATE	TOTAL	DATE	TOTAL
DATE	TOTAL	DATE	TOTAL
DATE	TOTAL	DATE	TOTAL
DATE	TOTAL	DATE	TOTAL
DATE	TOTAL	DATE	TOTAL
DATE	TOTAL	DATE	TOTAL
DATE	TOTAL	DATE	TOTAL
DATE	TOTAL	DATE	TOTAL
DATE	TOTAL	DATE	TOTAL
DATE	TOTAL	DATE	TOTAL
DATE	TOTAL	DATE	TOTAL
DATE	TOTAL	DATE	TOTAL
DATE	TOTAL	DATE	TOTAL
DATE	TOTAL	DATE	TOTAL

Backyard Big Year

DATE	TOTAL	DATE	TOTAL
DATE	TOTAL	DATE	TOTAL
DATE	TOTAL	DATE	TOTAL
DATE	TOTAL	DATE	TOTAL
DATE	TOTAL	DATE	TOTAL
DATE	TOTAL	DATE	TOTAL
DATE	TOTAL	DATE	TOTAL
DATE	TOTAL	DATE	TOTAL
DATE	TOTAL	DATE	TOTAL
DATE	TOTAL	DATE	TOTAL
DATE	TOTAL	DATE	TOTAL
DATE	TOTAL	DATE	TOTAL
DATE	TOTAL	DATE	TOTAL
DATE	TOTAL	DATE	TOTAL

Backyard Big Year

DATE	TOTAL	DATE	TOTAL
DATE	TOTAL	DATE	TOTAL
DATE	TOTAL	DATE	TOTAL
DATE	TOTAL	DATE	TOTAL
DATE	TOTAL	DATE	TOTAL
DATE	TOTAL	DATE	TOTAL
DATE	TOTAL	DATE	TOTAL
DATE	TOTAL	DATE	TOTAL
DATE	TOTAL	DATE	TOTAL
DATE	TOTAL	DATE	TOTAL
DATE	TOTAL	DATE	TOTAL
DATE	TOTAL	DATE	TOTAL
DATE	TOTAL	DATE	TOTAL
DATE	TOTAL	DATE	TOTAL
DATE	TOTAL	DATE	TOTAL

Backyard Big Year

DATE	TOTAL	DATE	TOTAL
DATE	TOTAL	DATE	TOTAL
DATE	TOTAL	DATE	TOTAL
DATE	TOTAL	DATE	TOTAL
DATE	TOTAL	DATE	TOTAL
DATE	TOTAL	DATE	TOTAL
DATE	TOTAL	DATE	TOTAL
DATE	TOTAL	DATE	TOTAL
DATE	TOTAL	DATE	TOTAL
DATE	TOTAL	DATE	TOTAL
DATE	TOTAL	DATE	TOTAL
DATE	TOTAL	DATE	TOTAL
DATE	TOTAL	DATE	TOTAL
DATE	TOTAL	DATE	TOTAL

Backyard Big Day

DATE	TOTAL		DATE	TOTAL
DATE	TOTAL		DATE	TOTAL
DATE	TOTAL		DATE	TOTAL
DATE	TOTAL		DATE	TOTAL
DATE	TOTAL		DATE	TOTAL
DATE	TOTAL		DATE	TOTAL
DATE	TOTAL		DATE	TOTAL
DATE	TOTAL		DATE	TOTAL
DATE	TOTAL		DATE	TOTAL
DATE	TOTAL		DATE	TOTAL
DATE	TOTAL		DATE	TOTAL
DATE	TOTAL		DATE	TOTAL
DATE	TOTAL		DATE	TOTAL
DATE	TOTAL		DATE	TOTAL

Backyard Big Day

DATE	TOTAL	DATE	TOTAL
DATE	TOTAL	DATE	TOTAL
DATE	TOTAL	DATE	TOTAL
DATE	TOTAL	DATE	TOTAL
DATE	TOTAL	DATE	TOTAL
DATE	TOTAL	DATE	TOTAL
DATE	TOTAL	DATE	TOTAL
DATE	TOTAL	DATE	TOTAL
DATE	TOTAL	DATE	TOTAL
DATE	TOTAL	DATE	TOTAL
DATE	TOTAL	DATE	TOTAL
DATE	TOTAL	DATE	TOTAL
DATE	TOTAL	DATE	TOTAL
DATE	TOTAL	DATE	TOTAL
DATE	TOTAL	DATE	TOTAL

Backyard Nesting Birds

1
2
3
4
5
6
7
8
9
10
11
12
13
14
15

16
17
18
19
20
21
22
23
24
25
26
27
28
29
30

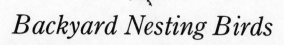

Backyard Nesting Birds

31 _____

32 _____

33 _____

34 _____

35 _____

36 _____

37 _____

38 _____

39 _____

40 _____

41 _____

42 _____

43 _____

44 _____

45 _____

46 _____

47 _____

48 _____

49 _____

50 _____

51 _____

52 _____

53 _____

54 _____

55 _____

56 _____

57 _____

58 _____

59 _____

60 _____

Backyard Nesting Birds

61 _____

62 _____

63 _____

64 _____

65 _____

66 _____

67 _____

68 _____

69 _____

70 _____

71 _____

72 _____

73 _____

74 _____

75 _____

76 _____

77 _____

78 _____

79 _____

80 _____

81 _____

82 _____

83 _____

84 _____

85 _____

86 _____

87 _____

88 _____

89 _____

90 _____

Backyard Nesting Birds

91 _____

92 _____

93 _____

94 _____

95 _____

96 _____

97 _____

98 _____

99 _____

100 _____

101 _____

102 _____

103 _____

104 _____

105 _____

106 _____

107 _____

108 _____

109 _____

110 _____

111 _____

112 _____

113 _____

114 _____

115 _____

116 _____

117 _____

118 _____

119 _____

120 _____

Backyard Christmas Count

DATE	TOTAL	DATE	TOTAL
DATE	TOTAL	DATE	TOTAL
DATE	TOTAL	DATE	TOTAL
DATE	TOTAL	DATE	TOTAL
DATE	TOTAL	DATE	TOTAL
DATE	TOTAL	DATE	TOTAL
DATE	TOTAL	DATE	TOTAL
DATE	TOTAL	DATE	TOTAL
DATE	TOTAL	DATE	TOTAL
DATE	TOTAL	DATE	TOTAL
DATE	TOTAL	DATE	TOTAL
DATE	TOTAL	DATE	TOTAL
DATE	TOTAL	DATE	TOTAL
DATE	TOTAL	DATE	TOTAL

Backyard Christmas Count

DATE	TOTAL	DATE	TOTAL
DATE	TOTAL	DATE	TOTAL
DATE	TOTAL	DATE	TOTAL
DATE	TOTAL	DATE	TOTAL
DATE	TOTAL	DATE	TOTAL
DATE	TOTAL	DATE	TOTAL
DATE	TOTAL	DATE	TOTAL
DATE	TOTAL	DATE	TOTAL
DATE	TOTAL	DATE	TOTAL
DATE	TOTAL	DATE	TOTAL
DATE	TOTAL	DATE	TOTAL
DATE	TOTAL	DATE	TOTAL
DATE	TOTAL	DATE	TOTAL
DATE	TOTAL	DATE	TOTAL

Backyard Christmas Count

DATE	TOTAL	DATE	TOTAL
DATE	TOTAL	DATE	TOTAL
DATE	TOTAL	DATE	TOTAL
DATE	TOTAL	DATE	TOTAL
DATE	TOTAL	DATE	TOTAL
DATE	TOTAL	DATE	TOTAL
DATE	TOTAL	DATE	TOTAL
DATE	TOTAL	DATE	TOTAL
DATE	TOTAL	DATE	TOTAL
DATE	TOTAL	DATE	TOTAL
DATE	TOTAL	DATE	TOTAL
DATE	TOTAL	DATE	TOTAL
DATE	TOTAL	DATE	TOTAL
DATE	TOTAL	DATE	TOTAL

Backyard Christmas Count

DATE	TOTAL	DATE	TOTAL

Backyard Rarities

1	DATE		16	DATE
2	DATE		17	DATE
3	DATE		18	DATE
4	DATE		19	DATE
5	DATE		20	DATE
6	DATE		21	DATE
7	DATE		22	DATE
8	DATE		23	DATE
9	DATE		24	DATE
10	DATE		25	DATE
11	DATE		26	DATE
12	DATE		27	DATE
13	DATE		28	DATE
14	DATE		29	DATE
15	DATE		30	DATE

Backyard Rarities

31 _____	DATE _____	46 _____	DATE _____
32 _____	DATE _____	47 _____	DATE _____
33 _____	DATE _____	48 _____	DATE _____
34 _____	DATE _____	49 _____	DATE _____
35 _____	DATE _____	50 _____	DATE _____
36 _____	DATE _____	51 _____	DATE _____
37 _____	DATE _____	52 _____	DATE _____
38 _____	DATE _____	53 _____	DATE _____
39 _____	DATE _____	54 _____	DATE _____
40 _____	DATE _____	55 _____	DATE _____
41 _____	DATE _____	56 _____	DATE _____
42 _____	DATE _____	57 _____	DATE _____
43 _____	DATE _____	58 _____	DATE _____
44 _____	DATE _____	59 _____	DATE _____
45 _____	DATE _____	60 _____	DATE _____

APPENDICES

Roger Tory Peterson's Backyard Life List

ROGER TORY PETERSON is one of the world's best known and honored naturalists. He is most noted for his innovative field guides, especially his *Field Guide to the Birds*, and his lifelong involvement with birds. His passion for and understanding of all living organisms, plant or animal, are evident in everything he does—driving through the countryside in search of wildflowers, birding in Alaska, or working in his backyard in Old Lyme, Connecticut, where he has dug a pond and planted a butterfly garden.

When I called Roger, asking him if he would share his Backyard Life List, he agreed but cautioned me that several of the birds on his list, like the Upland Sandpiper, were heard at night, overhead. He wanted to make sure we were both using the same criteria for a Backyard List, which we were. All that is required is identification; how one goes about it depends on a birder's ability and inclination. The average backyard birder won't find himself identifying birds in the dark. Learning to identify a bird's call as it flies over at night is not a readily acquired skill. Beginning in his teenage years, Roger has put in a lifetime of birding. He has birded at his present residence in Old Lyme for thirty-two years. If a bird of note is within hearing or seeing distance and if Roger is at home and awake, day or night, the bird will make it to Roger's Backyard List.

Roger Tory Peterson and his wife, Virginia Marie Peterson, live on seventy-one acres of mostly oak-covered ridge. They also have a brackish marsh and swamp on their property, giving them such birds as Virginia Rail, Sora, and nesting Green-backed Herons.

They have several tubular feeders filled with sunflower seed. Suet is put out during the winter, and they scatter wild seed mix on the ground near their home and Roger's studio.

Roger has seen several species come and go throughout the thirty-two years. American Woodcock and Brown Thrasher are gone because of habitat loss as the woodlands matured. Whip-poor-will is gone because of the disappearance of the large saturnid moth. Roger thinks that spraying for the gypsy moth could explain saturnid's disappearance. Red-shouldered Hawk, Barred Owl, and Louisiana Waterthrush resided on the property across from him until the construction of a small development of homes. He has several newcomers to his backyard: Northern Cardinal, Tufted Titmouse, and Red-bellied Woodpecker. His Mourning Dove population has increased throughout the years.

Roger Tory Peterson's Backyard Life List numbers 152 species. Of these, 68 have bred; 52 have bred regularly.

Double-crested Cormorant—OV
Great Blue Heron—OV
Great Egret—SR
Snowy Egret—SR
Green-backed Heron—SR-N
Black-crowned Night Heron—OV
Canada Goose—OV
Wood Duck—SR
American Black Duck—SR
Mallard—PR
Common Goldeneye—OV
Common Merganser—OV
Turkey Vulture—OV
Osprey—SR-N (no longer nests)
Bald Eagle—OV
Sharp-shinned Hawk—O
Cooper's Hawk—O
Northern Goshawk—Ra
Red-shouldered Hawk—N-NLS
Broad-winged Hawk—SR-N
Red-tailed Hawk—O
Ring-necked Pheasant—PR-O
Ruffed Grouse—PR-N
Wild Turkey—PR-ON
Northern Bobwhite—PR-N
Virginia Rail—SR-N
Sora—SR
Black-bellied Plover—OV
Killdeer—OV
Greater Yellowlegs—MT-OV
Solitary Sandpiper—MT-Ra
Spotted Sandpiper—MT-Ra
Upland Sandpiper—OV (night)
Whimbrel—OV

American Woodcock—SR-N (no
    longer nests)
Laughing Gull—OV
Ringed-billed Gull—OV
Herring Gull—OV
Great Black-backed Gull—OV
Rock Dove—PR-N
Mourning Dove—PR-N
Black-billed Cuckoo—SR-N
Yellow-billed Cuckoo—SR-N
Eastern Screech-Owl—Ra
Great Horned Owl—PR-N
    (probable)
Barred Owl—PR-N (probable)
Long-eared Owl—Ra
Common Nighthawk—MT-OV
Whip-poor-will—N-NLS
Chimney Swift—SR-OV
Ruby-throated Hummingbird—SR-N
Belted Kingfisher—Ra
Red-bellied Woodpecker—N
    (probable)
Yellow-bellied Sapsucker—O-Sp
Downy Woodpecker—PR-N
Hairy Woodpecker—PR-N
Northern (Yellow-shafted) Flicker—
    SR-N
Pileated Woodpecker—Ra
Eastern Wood-Pewee—SR
Yellow-bellied Flycatcher—MT-Ra
Eastern Phoebe—SR-N (no longer
    nests)
Great Crested Flycatcher—SR-N
Eastern Kingbird—SR

Purple Martin—MT-OV
Tree Swallow—MT-OV
Northern Rough-winged Swallow—
    MT-OV
Bank Swallow—MT-OV
Cliff Swallow—MT
Barn Swallow—MT-OV
Blue Jay—PR-N
American Crow—PR-N
Fish Crow—O
Black-capped Chickadee—PR-N
Tufted Titmouse—PR-N
Red-breasted Nuthatch—WR-O
White-breasted Nuthatch—PR-N
Brown Creeper—WR
Carolina Wren—SR-N
House Wren—SR-N
Winter Wren—O
Marsh Wren—SR-N (probable)
Golden-crowned Kinglet—WR
Ruby-crowned Kinglet—MT
Eastern Bluebird—MT-OV
Veery—SR-N
Swainson's Thrush—MT
Hermit Thrush—MT
Wood Thrush—SR-N
American Robin—SR-N
Gray Catbird—SR-N
Brown Thrasher—N-NLS
Cedar Waxwing—ON
European Starling—Ra
Solitary Vireo—MT
Yellow-throated Vireo—SR-N
    (probable)

Red-eyed Vireo—SR-N
Blue-winged Warbler—SR-N
Golden-winged Warbler—MT-Ra
Nashville Warbler—MT
Northern Parula—SR-N (probable)
Yellow Warbler—SR-ON
Chestnut-sided Warbler—SR-N (no
    longer nests)
Magnolia Warbler—MT
Yellow-rumped (Myrtle) Warbler—
    MT, WR-Ra
Black-throated Green Warbler—SR-
    N (probable)
Blackburnian Warbler—MT
Pine Warbler—MT-Ra
Prairie Warbler—SR-N
Palm Warbler—MT
Bay-breasted Warbler—MT
Blackpoll Warbler—MT
Black-and-white Warbler—SR-N
American Redstart—MT-Ra
Worm-eating Warbler—SR-N

Ovenbird—SR-N
Northern Waterthrush—MT
Louisiana Waterthrush—SR (may
    still nest)
Mourning Warbler—MT
Common Yellowthroat—SR-N
Hooded Warbler—SR-N
Canada Warbler—MT
Scarlet Tanager—SR-N
Northern Cardinal—PR-N
Rose-breasted Grosbeak—SR-N
Indigo Bunting—SR-ON
Dickcissel—OV (night)
Rufous-sided Towhee—SR-N, WR-
    O
American Tree Sparrow—WR
    (becoming scarce)
Chipping Sparrow—SR (no longer
    nests)
Field Sparrow—WV-O
Fox Sparrow—MT, WR-O
Song Sparrow—PR-N

Swamp Sparrow—SR-N
White-throated Sparrow—WR
White-crowned Sparrow—Ra (one
    record)
Dark-eyed (Slate-colored) Junco—
    WR
Bobolink—MT-OV (night)
Red-winged Blackbird—SR-N
Rusty Blackbird—MT
Common Grackle—SR-N
Brown-headed Cowbird—SR-N
Northern Oriole—SR-N
Pine Grosbeak—WV-Ra
Purple Finch—SR-N (probable)
House Finch—PR-N
Red Crossbill—WV-Ra
White-winged Crossbill—WV-Ra
Common Redpoll—WV-Ra
Pine Siskin—WR-O
American Goldfinch—PR-N
Evening Grosbeak—WV-O
House Sparrow—SV-Ra

BINOCULARS AND FIELD GUIDES

YOUR BINOCULARS and field guide are the two most-considered purchases you'll have to make to get you in touch with your backyard birds. Since the mechanics of binoculars are on the complicated side and binoculars themselves are expensive, you should know what to look for before you go off to shop. Field guides are inexpensive, but they have their own peculiarities, like binoculars, and a novice, before cracking open his first field guide, could stand a light primer on their history, differences, and pluses and minuses. Besides, the field guide has, without fanfare, headlines, national acclaim, or cataclysmic interruption of our daily business, sparked a nation's perception and sensitivity to the natural world; its inception takes its place in history along with the wheel and the computer chip. So it is important that we make a little fuss about this field guide you are about to buy. It's hard to imagine life without it.

Binoculars

You want center-focus binoculars because they're quick and easy to focus, and they can focus as close as ten feet. There are two center-focus designs to choose from—the standard porro prism, which is the most common, and the roof prism. They differ in the arrangement of their prisms, and each has its advantages and disadvantages, depending on one's point of view of the world and the size of one's pocketbook.

The standard porro prism binocs have their optics offset and consequently are chunkier than the roof prisms, but the chunkiness offers a place for a firm grip. The roof prism binocs have their optics arranged in a straight line, allowing for a straight, slender barrel and a compact, lightweight binocular. They give you superb resolution without loss of brightness or field of view, but they don't focus as close as the standard prism and they have no depth of field to speak of; the standard prism has depth of field.

When one says that a binocular has depth of field, it means that when you focus on a bird the immediate foreground and background will also be in focus, so if your bird shifts forward or back you won't have to refocus; with a roof prism you will—no great hardship though. Roof prisms are also very expensive to buy and repair—possibly a hardship.

Power. On the flat surface of a binocular's housing you'll find three numbers, such as: 7 × 35 7.5. The first number, 7×, designates the binocular's power. Seven power increases the size of a bird seven times, eight power eight times, and so on. Any power above

$10\times$ is not for you. You'll find it difficult to keep an image steady because not only is the magnification increased but also any movements you might make, like breathing. Most birders use a $7\times$ or $8\times$. I have a $9\times$ and have no problem holding it steady.

Brightness.   The second number, *35*, has to do with the amount of light that enters the binocular. It represents the diameter in millimeters of the objective lens, which is the receiving end of the binocular. The larger the objective lens, the more light. The more light, the brighter the image and greater its detail. Working in tandem with the objective lens, also determining brightness and quality of image, is the exit pupil, located at the viewing end. It is a tiny round hole measured in millimeters, through which the light passes to your eyes. The size of the exit pupil can be found on the binocular's spec sheet, or you can compute it by dividing the size of the objective lens by the magnification number. Keep in mind that the larger numbers shed more light on details at low light levels, as on a cloudy day and at dusk. From 30 to 40 are good numbers for an objective lens. From 3.5 to 5 mm are good numbers for the exit pupil.

Field of View.   The third number, *7.5*, designates the field of view in degrees, which has to be expressed in feet per 1000 yards before it will make any sense; that is, number of feet a binocular encompasses at 1000 yards. The more feet it encompasses, the wider your field of view and the greater chance you have, when you snap those binoculars up to your eyes, of nailing that elusive warbler before it disappears into the foliage. Your binocular's spec sheet includes the field of view, but you can also compute it. We know that 52.5 feet equal 1 degree at 1000 yards. If you take the degrees indicated on the binocular, in our example 7.5, and multiply this figure by 52.5 you will arrive at the field of view, which is 380 feet of area seen at 1000 yards. A field of view of 360 to 400 feet at 1000 yards is what you should be looking for. Don't be tempted to go for extremely wide-angle binoculars because they are expensive, bulky, and won't add anything to your birding pleasure.

Manufacturers.   Nikon, Pentax, Minolta, and Bushnell offer an excellent selection of binoculars for a variety of budgets. Zeiss and Leitz are known for their roof prisms, superb quality, and superb price. Several new interesting-looking manufacturers consistently spend their advertising dollars in *Audubon* magazine; pick up a copy and see what else is available.

Note: Most prices can be discounted. Look for ads in popular camera magazines. But don't spend less than $60 or you will be sorry. Some manufacturers offer extras, like binocular casings designed for people who wear glasses, or optics that allow complete visibility while wearing glasses.

Spotting Scopes

If your home overlooks a beach, marsh, body of water, meadow, or any vista, you can use more power than your binoculars can muster. A spotting scope is what you need, and $20\times$ is the answer to your forthcoming question, What power spotting scope? Twenty power is the best all-purpose magnification, giving you the details even on an overcast day and not giving you hazy and shimmering images on a bright, sunny day. You'll need a tripod to hold the scope steady, preferably a flip-lock tripod for ease of operation. A spring-loaded vertical-angle control will keep your scope from flopping down when the control is loosened. Busnell and Nikon both carry quality scopes.

And then there is the Questar—a small, lightweight field telescope with a reflecting rather than a refracting lens, capable of extreme magnifications ($40\times$, $60\times$, $80\times$, and up) without noticeable loss of sharpness and light even at low light levels. The Questar delivers the light because of its 89-mm objective lens. If your backyard hasn't enough vista to warrant a magnification of more than a $10 \times$ binocular, the Questar telescope can still give you a reason to spend up to $1700. You see—and you will see—the Questar focuses down to 10 feet; which means the image through a Questar at 10 feet with $60 \times$ magnification is equivalent to placing one of your winter birds at the feeder under a microscope, as you would a one-celled amoeba, and magnifying it beyond actual size, larger than life, for your scrutiny.

Field Guides

Historic Moments in Field Guides.   Roger Tory Peterson's *Field Guide to the Birds* was published in 1934. His guide revolutionized birding, providing birders with a clear, pragmatic system of identifying birds in the field. His guide was responsible for the proliferation of birders to come, for a growing public awareness of the avifauna and environment, and concurrently, for bolstering the health of the binocular industry. For twenty-nine years birders religiously carried their Petersons into the field. For twenty-nine years the guide reigned supreme. Then in 1966, that all changed. Golden Books published its *Birds of North America*. Suddenly loyalties were strained. Now birders had a choice, and birders never had it so good.

Peterson's *Field Guide to the Birds*.   There are three volumes of Peterson's *Field Guide to the Birds*, published by Houghton Mifflin: one covering birds east of the Rockies, one western birds, and one the birds of Texas. Typically, one page is devoted to illustrations, and the facing page is devoted to succinct text describing a species' field marks, song, range, and habitat. There is a short paragraph titled "Similar Species," telling you how to discriminate between lookalikes; that is one of the guide's strong points but not *the* strong point. What makes the guide what it was back then and what it still is today is the Peterson system, which is, as described in the guide's own introduction, "based on patternistic drawings with arrows that pinpoint the key field marks."

"Patternistic," even though it is an apt description of Peterson's bird illustrations, doesn't do them justice and is misleading. What makes Peterson's field guide special, what makes it work, besides the flagging of field marks, is his interpretation and rendering of these field marks. Certain birds, like shorebirds and sparrows, are much more difficult to interpret and render than other birds; the illustrations in field guides usually reflect the difficulty by the shortcuts an illustrator has taken. Not so with Peterson; the complicated mottling, barring, striping, streaking are thoughtfully interpreted and carefully rendered. For each "formal schematic illustration," as the guide calls them, Peterson has managed to faithfully represent the bird by keeping a proper balance and relationship between color, value, line, pattern, and form.

In an effort to accent and clarify field marks Peterson has enhanced the bird. A Peterson's bird always looks its best and captures the essence of the species it represents. The result is a superrealism, part schematic illustration, part Rousseau painting. The result is enticement and ease of identification. Peterson's birds translate from the page to the field with minimal confusion and difficulty; no other guide does the job as well. Overhead patterns, flight patterns, fall and winter plumages, immature plumages, and silhouettes are also part of Peterson's system and are important aids in field identification.

Birds of North America.   Golden Books and four men, Chandler S. Robbins, Bertel Bruun, Herbert S. Zim, and illustrator Arthur Singer, are responsible for this guide. It is an outstanding achievement and quite a piece of work. What makes this field guide the success it is?

The guide, as its name indicates, consolidated all the North American birds under one cover. So a birder needs only one guide to carry into the field no matter where that field might happen to be. And the field guide has a birder covered; if a nonregional, unrecognizable vagrant blows his way, he knows he's going to find it somewhere among the 325 pages. And as a birder looks up one bird from his side of the Rockies, he can, by association, become familiar with related species on the other side of the Rockies. The guide provides a compact introduction to the birds available in North America and possibly could incite wanderlust.

The text, on the page opposite the illustrations, is short, giving field marks and, when appropriate, song, habitat, and diagnostic traits. It doesn't have to mention a species' range because next to the text for each bird is a small, color-keyed map of North America, showing at a glance the winter, summer, and permanent ranges of the bird and, if a migrant, its route and spring arrival dates. If a birder had any doubt whether the bird he sighted was supposed to be where he sighted it, all he'd have to do is take a look at the map. The range map is a major innovation and a quick study.

The guide has also introduced the sonagram, a visual representation of a bird's song, showing frequency and pattern. Sonagrams still aren't as effective as verbal descriptions, and I would wager that most birders make little use of them. But if one used the sonagram in conjunction with a recorded bird song it would eventually make some sense.

Arthur Singer, the illustrator, often incorporates a part of the environment and habitat with each bird illustration; he tells us where a bird lives by the use of a twig, branch, leaf, or flower, by a nest, the berry in a bird's bill, or the bark of a tree the bird is clinging to. On the same page, along with the birds and their habitats, Singer includes different plumages, and flight patterns when necessary. He has successfully managed to squeeze an enormous amount of visual information onto one page. The field guide is an incredible feat of design and organization and has more than made use of the phrase "A picture is worth a thousand words."

Recommending a Field Guide.   So where do we come out as far as the two field guides go? Peterson's field guide is ideal for the novice birder and also the backyard birder. His revised *Field Guide to the Birds of Eastern and Central North America*, fourth edition, now carries range maps, and soon his western guide also will; the range maps are located in the rear of the book and will take several seconds to get to. It is safe to say that every serious birder has a copy of Robbins's *Birds of North America*. Most birders own both. So that's my recommendation. Get both. Use Peterson's to learn with and thumb through Robbins's for the larger picture.

Now, to add to the dilemma, National Geographic has introduced its *Field Guide to the Birds of North America*. It is patterned after Robbins and offers nothing that hasn't been covered by Robbins and Peterson, but the illustrations, exceptionally executed for a field guide, are considered by many birding experts to be the most accurate and can provide reason enough to purchase the guide. Call National Geographic's toll-free order number if you're interested: 800-638-4077.

I would like to introduce you to one more field guide, *The Audubon Society Master Guide to Birding*, published by Knopf and edited by John Farrand, Jr. It comes in three volumes and is designed for the serious birder. The text is written by the nation's top field ornithologists and experts. Most of the birds, in several plumages, are represented by exceptional color photography, which in turn is represented by exceptional reproduction. Fine bird illustrations also supplement the text, and the guide's only fault is its illegible range maps. After several years of backyard birding you might want to consider it for your library. The color photography provides you with a fresh visual reference and the text with some of the finer points of field identification.

ATTRACTING BIRDS TO YOUR BACKYARD

FOR MAXIMUM yield of birds, your backyard has to provide adequate food, shelter, and water. Some backyards are endowed with all three; some need a boost. No matter how much your backyard has to offer, nothing attracts the birds like a feeder chock-full of birdseed.

The Feeder

The latest innovation and the most popular feeder today is the tubular feeder. It consists of a vertically hung tube, usually clear plastic, with open seed slots on the side and small rods for birds to perch on and feed from. The feeder is enclosed top and bottom, protecting the seeds, and usually requires less refilling than other feeders. It can be hung or fixed on a pole but is usually seen hanging. This feeder favors smaller birds, like chickadees, titmouses, and finches, and only the more determined, less shy, dexterous larger birds can manage to perch and feed at the same time. If you want to make sure your ground-foraging birds and larger birds get their share, don't use the plastic plate that attaches to the bottom of the feeder: without it enough seed will be tossed to the ground by the birds at the feeder to provide for those birds below the feeder. If you want to cater to the larger birds (cardinals, blue jays, blackbirds), set out a platform feeder. It works with and without a roof and has sides to protect the seeds; it can be hung, put on a pole, or placed on the ground. Feeders come in a multitude of designs and shapes and have their accessories, like squirrel and predator prevention devices. Go through the feeder catalogues. You'll be amazed.

Placing the Feeder

For your convenience, comfort, and pleasure, decide what room or rooms you want to lie back and watch the birds from, and place your feeder accordingly. Hang it from a tree or fix it on a pole, but place it near some shelter and shrubs for birds to perch on and survey their approach from. Friends of mine who live in Woodstock, New York, strategically place their feeders and other enticeables throughout their outdoor patio. Subsequently, every spring and fall as they sit outside at their patio table, chickadees zip between their ear lobe and shoulder, titmouses and nuthatches dangle three feet over their head, and woodpeckers, among others, dine five feet from their morning cup of coffee.

Wild Bird Seed Mix

Wild bird seed mixes are supposed to appeal to a variety of backyard birds. You will soon discover that with any seed mix certain birds will eagerly feast on some fraction of it while avoiding others. Following is a description of what goes into a mix and which bird is supposed to prefer what. Keep in mind that a wild bird seed mix is a supplement for weed and wildflower seed that make up the natural food supply of most wintering birds, that food preferences typical for one area will not always hold true for another, and that for every mix the ratio of seed types varies from supplier to supplier. One should always check out the contents and proportions of a mix to make sure it's compatible with the appetites of your backyard birds.

Sunflower Seed.   Sunflower seed is a must. If you want to see nuthatches, chickadees, titmouses, Pine Siskins, and Evening Grosbeaks, among other notables, your wild seed mix will have to include sunflower seed; most usually do. It is the only component in the mix that is not a grass seed, and it is usually a smaller fraction; some suppliers carry a wild bird seed mix with sunflower seed as the dominant fraction. You can buy separate bags of sunflower seed. Many people keep one feeder filled with just sunflower seed, but when I tried it the sunflower feeder was depleted within the day and my mixed-seed feeder was ignored.

Millet or Prolo Millet.   Millet is a small grass seed found in better seed mixes. It is a preferred food of small ground-feeding birds like sparrows, juncos, towhees, and Mourning Doves. Millet comes in white or red. There are those who say the birds prefer the white millet. Others say millet is millet. It should be the largest single component in better wild seed mixes unless you specify sunflower seed.

Sorghum or Milo.   Sorghum, or milo, is a cheaper grass seed than millet, and you'll find more of it in cheaper wild seed mixes. It is not a preferred food of smaller birds but your medium-sized birds such as grackles, jays, and Mourning Doves won't turn it away.

Wheat and Corn.   Wheat and corn are less-preferred foods, but will do in a pinch. Cracked corn is fed upon by some smaller birds, like sparrows and juncos. Coarser grades are taken by jays, crows, waterfowl, pheasants and wild turkeys.

Expanding the Menu

Niger or Thistle.   Niger, or thistle, is never part of a wild seed mix. It is considered gourmet by the smaller finches such as goldfinches, Pine Siskins, redpolls, and so on. This small seed comes from India or Ethiopia and is the most expensive seed on the market. Niger, or thistle, belongs to the sunflower family, but because of its smaller size it requires a tubular feeder with smaller seed slots, called a thistle feeder.

Suet.   Suet is animal fat. On extremely cold days woodpeckers, nuthatches, chickadees, Brown Creepers, and titmouses all could use some suet in their diet, and none of these birds will turn it away. There was a time in the meat departments of most supermarkets when you could get your suet free for the asking. Today the supermarkets are wise to the ways of the backyard birder and have their suet packaged, priced, and displayed. Hang your suet outside in suet feeders, special wire baskets, or nylon bags. You can find them in any bird-feeding catalogue.

From the Kitchen.   Birds also like peanut butter, bread crumbs, nuts, and fruit. Stick the fruit on a branch; spread the peanut butter on a pine cone.

Bird Feeder Study

Following is a summary of various species' preferred foods, as determined in a 1978–1984 study made by the Chicago Audubon Society and their research committee chairman, Alan Anderson. Their data were collected from feeders in and about the Chicago area for six Chicago winters. Even though the study is regional, it represents the food preferences of 60 species, several of which are likely to be found in your backyard.

Bird Feeds and the Birds They Attract

I. Corn

Species	No. feeders	Abundant	Appearance at feeders Common	Unusual	Rare
House Sparrow	25	19	5	1	0
Mourning Dove	19	10	7	1	1
Eur. Starling	17	8	1	2	6
N. Cardinal	17	8	7	1	1
Dark-eyed Junco	16	10	3	2	1
Blue Jay	12	6	3	2	1
Ring-nkd. Pheasant	10	5	3	1	1
Common Crow	10	4	5	1	0
Common Grackle	7	3	2	2	0
Tree Sparrow	7	0	5	2	0
Blk.-cpd. Chickadee	7	2	3	2	0
Red-winged Blackbird	6	2	3	1	0
Mallard	5	2	1	1	1
White-thr. Sparrow	3	0	1	1	1
N. Flicker	3	0	3	0	0
Brown-hd. Cowbird	2	1	1	0	0
Rock Dove	2	1	1	0	0
Song Sparrow	2	0	1	1	0

(Species seen by only one person at a single feeder included: Black Duck, Canada Goose, American Goldfinch, White-crowned Sparrow, Swamp Sparrow, and White-breasted Nuthatch.)

II. Sunflower

Species	No. feeders	Abundant	Appearance at feeders Common	Unusual	Rare
Blk.-cpd. Chickadee	135	89	28	13	5
N. Cardinal	106	53	30	16	7
House Sparrow	91	40	24	17	10
American Goldfinch	70	37	20	7	6
Dark-eyed Junco	63	28	22	9	4
Mourning Dove	39	11	11	15	2
Blue Jay	35	4	9	14	8
Purple Finch	37	18	11	3	5
Eur. Starling	26	8	5	6	7
White-breasted Nuthatch	34	13	12	5	4
Downy Woodpecker	28	1	11	12	4
Common Grackle	24	10	6	5	3
Tree Sparrow	27	3	9	8	7
Pine Siskin	24	13	2	6	3
Common Redpoll	19	8	4	4	3
Fox Sparrow	17	7	4	3	3
Red-winged Blackbird	13	3	5	2	3
Rock Dove	12	3	1	4	4
N. Flicker	9	0	4	4	1
Tufted Titmouse	8	1	3	1	3
Evening Grosbeak	5	0	1	1	4
Song Sparrow	5	1	2	1	1
Red-bellied Woodpecker	4	1	1	1	1
Common Crow	4	0	1	2	1
American Robin	3	1	0	0	2
Fox Sparrow	3	0	0	1	2
Hairy Woodpecker	2	0	1	1	0
Red-headed Woodpecker	3	0	0	3	0

(Species seen by only one person at a single feeder included: Rose-breasted Grosbeak, Brown-headed Cowbird, Rufous-sided Towhee, White-crowned Sparrow, and White-throated Sparrow.)

III. Thistle

Species	No. feeders	Abundant	Appearance at feeders Common	Unusual	Rare
American Goldfinch	112	71	22	12	7
Blk.-cpd. Chickadee	63	21	13	12	17
Dark-eyed Junco	55	23	14	12	6
Common Redpoll	35	16	7	5	7
House Sparrow	29	5	8	7	8
Pine Siskin	31	14	7	6	4
Mourning Dove	24	13	8	3	0
Purple Finch	18	1	4	9	4
Tree Sparrow	16	1	4	6	5
N. Cardinal	8	1	3	0	4
White-breasted Nuthatch	4	2	0	2	0
Song Sparrow	3	0	0	3	0
Common Grackle	2	1	0	0	1
Red-breasted Nuthatch	2	1	0	0	1
Rock Dove	2	0	1	0	1
White-throated Sparrow	2	0	0	1	1
Red-winged Blackbird	2	0	0	0	2
Swamp Sparrow	2	0	0	0	2

(Species seen by only one person at a single feeder included: Rufous-sided Towhee, European Starling, Brown-headed Cowbird, and White-winged Crossbill.)

IV. Suet

Species	No. feeders	Abundant	Appearance at feeders Common	Unusual	Rare
Downy Woodpecker	120	64	26	22	8
Blk.-cpd. Chickadee	85	42	23	15	5
Eur. Starling	69	24	14	17	14
Hairy Woodpecker	44	13	15	8	8
White-breasted Nuthatch	47	16	18	9	4
Blue Jay	24	3	9	6	6
Red-bellied Woodpecker	25	7	16	1	1
Dark-eyed Junco	20	10	6	1	3
American Goldfinch	23	6	3	5	9
N. Flicker	14	0	4	3	7
Red-breasted Nuthatch	15	4	4	2	5
Common Grackle	14	0	5	7	2
Common Crow	14	0	5	2	7
N. Cardinal	13	1	1	6	5
House Sparrow	12	3	1	5	3
Red-headed Woodpecker	10	1	4	5	0
Red-winged Blackbird	8	0	1	4	3
Tufted Titmouse	6	4	0	0	2
Purple Finch	6	5	1	0	0
Song Sparrow	4	1	0	2	1
Brown Creeper	4	0	0	0	4
Brown-hd. Cowbird	4	0	1	2	1
Yellow-bel. Sapsucker	3	1	0	0	2
Tree Sparrow	2	1	0	0	1
Mourning Dove	2	0	2	0	0
Evening Grosbeak	2	0	0	0	2

(Species seen by only one person at a single feeder included: Brown Thrasher, Common Redpoll, Pine Siskin, and Golden-crowned Kinglet.)

V. Mixed Seed

Species	No. feeders	Abundant	Appearance at feeders Common	Unusual	Rare
N. Cardinal	300	149	73	57	21
House Sparrow	313	237	56	8	12
Dark-eyed Junco	272	152	70	37	13
Blk.-cpd. Chickadee	229	99	68	31	31
Mourning Dove	173	61	58	32	22
Blue Jay	173	35	47	46	45
Eur. Starling	149	46	49	21	33
Tree Sparrow	126	45	39	17	25
American Goldfinch	86	17	19	24	26
Red-winged Blackbird	84	25	27	12	20
Rock Dove	62	27	14	13	8

V. Mixed Seed (continued)

Species	No. feeders	Abundant	Appearance at feeders Common	Unusual	Rare
Song Sparrow	61	13	22	13	13
White-breasted Nuthatch	58	16	22	9	11
Common Crow	44	2	11	14	17
Brown-hd. Cowbird	54	4	15	20	15
Downy Woodpecker	43	11	8	14	10
Purple Finch	38	4	9	13	12
White-throated Sparrow	36	10	4	8	14
Red-bellied Woodpecker	32	12	11	7	2
Pine Siskin	22	4	7	6	5
American Robin	18	1	3	5	9
Common Redpoll	22	2	5	1	14
N. Flicker	19	1	2	7	9
Ring-necked Pheasant	23	6	5	5	7
Tufted Titmouse	17	1	6	4	6
Fox Sparrow	17	0	4	4	9
Evening Grosbeak	17	1	2	1	13
Red-breasted Nuthatch	11	0	1	6	4
White-crowned Sparrow	13	2	2	0	9
Hairy Woodpecker	9	4	1	2	2
Swamp Sparrow	9	0	3	5	1
Red-headed Woodpecker	7	0	0	4	3
Mallard	4	1	1	1	1
Rufous-sided Towhee	3	1	0	0	2
Brown Creeper	3	0	0	1	2
Horned Lark	3	1	1	0	1
Monk Parakeet	3	1	0	0	2
Brown Thrasher	2	2	0	0	0
Bobwhite	2	0	2	0	0
Lapland Longspur	2	0	1	0	1

(Species seen by only one person at a single feeder included: Snow Bunting, Black-throated Sparrow, Hermit Thrush, Pine Grosbeak, and Cedar Waxwing.)

VI: Number of species reported taking each type of food, during each study year.

Year	Total No. Species	Sunflower	Species Reported Taking: Mixed	Thistle	Suet	Corn
1978–79	35	21	30	10	22	11
1979–80	36	15	35	6	12	8
1980–81	38	23	32	11	21	18
1981–82	55	24	42	17	27	14
1982–83	37	23	31	11	15	8
1983–84	42	21	27	12	15	11
Totals:	60	33	45	22	30	25
(Ave./Year:)	40	21	33	11	19	12

Definition of abundance terms.
Abundant: seen at feeder on an average of six or seven times a week. *Common*: seen at feeder on an average of three to five days a week. *Unusual*: seen at feeder on an average of once or twice a week. *Rare*: seen at feeder about one or two times a month.

Attracting Hummingbirds

Insects and flower nectar are the hummingbird's two major food sources. Insects are also attracted to nectar, so the more flowering plants in your backyard the more insects and the more provisions for your hummingbirds. Another way to attract hummingbirds is with a hummingbird feeder. There are a number of designs to select from. They are plastic, usually red, and try to resemble a flower. You'll find them in any bird-feeding catalogue. A simple formula for humming-bird nectar is one part granulated sugar to four parts water. Boil the water, add the sugar, stir and let cool. Store unused solution in the refrigerator. Fill the feeder as needed. Make sure you clean the feeder once a week with hot water plus a little vinegar to prevent mold. Scrub the feeder with a baby bottle brush and rinse thoroughly. (Note: do not add red food-coloring to the water.)

YOUR BACKYARD AS HABITAT

IN ECOLOGICAL terms, a community is an interacting, interlinking group of plant and animal species that lives in a particular environment. Three such communities are forest, prairie, and desert. Mankind has culled his backyard out of all three.

Within each community we find habitats, particular places to which a plant or animal is adapted and where it lives out part or all of its life cycle. Red-eyed Vireos live out their reproductive life cycle in a community of deciduous broadleaf forest; their habitat, the place they nest in and feed from, is amid the upper foliage, the forest canopy. Ovenbirds live in the same community but take advantage of a different habitat, the forest floor. We should think of our backyards in terms of the habitat available for our backyard birds.

Occasionally, a portion of a community is altered. A tornado sweeps through a two-hundred-acre tract of forest, creating an opening of twenty-five acres. This opening presents an opportunity for a new plant community to take hold, creating an incipient field or meadow with its own unique habitats and creatures. This fresh new opening, this clearing, has also created an edge, an important ecological concept that will give new meaning to your backyard.

An edge is a border between plant communities. The interface between the forest and the newly created opening is an edge. Certain plants are unique to an edge. Certain insects are unique to an edge.

Certain birds will exploit an edge. In many backyards throughout the United States we'll find an edge or semblance of one; that's where most of the action is going on as far as the birds and the backyard birders are concerned.

When humans move into a forest to build homes, they unwittingly create a number of edges. The road that abuts the forest and leads to home has an edge. The lawn and landscaping around the house create another. No doubt the backyard birding will be terrific because not only will birds from the interior of the woods—Wood Thrush, Red-eyed Vireo, Scarlet Tanager—visit the edge for food, there will also be those birds inhabiting the new community established at the edge—Blue-winged Warbler, Gray Catbird, Common Yellowthroat.

When man collectively sweeps through the forest, like our tornado, and creates suburbia in his wake, he also creates minihabitats and edges. There are those of us who are fortunate enough to live next to a forest or small woodlot where we can witness and enjoy the avian benefits of an edge. Often in the center of town or a large city we lose sight of the edge. Most urban gardens are a long way from the mother edge. But keep in mind that the edge is out there, someplace; it might be alongside a city park two blocks from your home or a forest preserve ten miles away; it could be a path of trees lining your block, guiding a wave of warblers to your backyard.

If your urban backyard has a few shrubs, a small garden, a tree or two, then you have a patch of miniedges with minihabitats for your resident birds, and you have a patch of green, attracting vagrants or migratory birds as they fly from one distant edge to another. Pine Siskins on their way from one woodlot to another might stop off at your feeder for a few days. All a Ruby-crowned Kinglet needs from your backyard before it continues on to its northern nesting grounds is a green shrub covered with droplets of water and insects swarming about it. An urban garden has possibilities, often surprises. An urban garden is an oasis among edifices, much like a suburb in a desert community is an oasis. They both provide their backyard birds with shelter, food, and water in an otherwise sparse environment. Both can attract a passing bird in need of a modicum of green teeming habitat.

Managing and Enhancing Your Habitat

Often aligning a woodlot, being part of the edge, are low shrubbery, briar patches, and bushy thickets where thicket-loving birds nest and feed. Any wild hedges such as these should be allowed to prosper; cut them back only to keep them from encroaching on your lawn, patio, and peace of mind. Several small shrubs and hedges, wild or ornamental, strategically planted throughout your lawn, provide habitat and create flyways from one edge to another. Leave dead trees stand if they don't present any danger to body, home, or electrical wires. Woodpeckers and some smaller birds nest in the cavities and hollows of dead trees, and the exterior surfaces of dead trees harbor all kinds of insect life for tree-climbing, trunk-pounding birds. Allow a portion of your lawn to grow wild; keep out the bushy thickets but let the grasses grow, the wildflowers and weeds take over; they'll provide seed, nectar, and insects for your backyard birds.

Planting the Right Shrub

The next time you take off to your local nursery to select a tree or shrub for your backyard, choose one that not only satisfies your taste but also the tastes of your backyard birds. Certain shrubs are known for their fruit, others for their nectar. Judicious selection and planting of these shrubs can keep your birds in food throughout the year. On page 289 you'll find a list of plants for different parts of the country and the birds they attract.

The Brush Pile

Create a minihabitat for insects, amphibians, reptiles, and rodents and a shelter and food source for your ground-foraging birds. If you can afford the space, construct a brush pile in your backyard, somewhere off in a corner or in between two plant communities, like the edge between your lawn and woodlot. Stack layers of branches and twigs, even toss in a discarded Christmas tree. Our brush pile houses Song Sparrow, White-throated Sparrow, Fox Sparrow, and Rufous-sided Towhee, to mention a few. Every fall, without fail, I'll find a Winter Wren bouncing in and out of its maze. This shelter becomes especially significant during the winter months. If you live in an area of heavy snowfall and low temperatures, the brush pile could be as important as your feeding stations. After a snowfall sweep it clean.

The Woodpile

If you keep a woodpile you won't be the only soul taking advantage of it during the winter months. Woodpiles develop natural communities of their own during the summer and fall. As you dig into it to

Bird-Attracting Shrubs

Region	Shrub	Fruit or Flower	Season	Birds Most Often Attracted
Northeast Connecticut	American Elder	Blue-black berries	Late summer to midfall	Bluebirds, Catbirds, Flickers, Mockingbirds, Rose-breasted Grosbeaks, Woodpeckers
Delaware Illinois Indiana	Amur Honeysuckle	Red berries	Fall to midwinter	Cardinals, Cedar Waxwings, Robins, Thrashers, Thrushes, Towhees, Winter Finches
Iowa	Arrowwood	Blue-black berries	Fall	Bluebirds, Catbirds, Flickers, Robins, Thrushes
Kentucky Maine Maryland	Bayberry	Gray berries	Fall to early spring	Bluebirds, Carolina Wrens, Downy Woodpeckers, Hermit Thrushes, Myrtle Warblers, Tree Swallows
Massachusetts Michigan Minnesota	Black Haw	Blue-black berries	Fall	Cedar Waxwings, Pileated Woodpeckers, Swainson's Thrushes, Yellow-billed Cuckoos
Missouri New Hampshire	High-bush Blueberry	Blue-black berries	Midsummer to midfall	Bluebirds, Chickadees, Hermit Thrushes, Orchard Orioles, Robins, Towhees
New Jersey New York Ohio	Nannyberry	Black berries	Fall	Catbirds, Cedar Waxwings, Flickers, Hermit Thrushes, Robins, Rose-breasted Grosbeaks
Ontario	Pinxter-bloom Azalea	Pink or white flowers	Spring	Ruby-throated Hummingbirds
Pennsylvania Quebec	Sargent Crab Apple	White flowers	Spring	Ruby-throated Hummingbirds
Rhode Island Vermont		Dark red fruit	Fall	Cedar Waxwings, Evening and Pine Grosbeaks, Purple Finches, Robins
Virginia West Virginia Wisconsin	Siberian Dogwood	Blue-white berries	Fall	Cardinals, Chats, Finches, Flycatchers, Mockingbirds, Tree Swallows
	Tatarian Honeysuckle	Pink or red flowers	Late spring	Ruby-throated Hummingbirds
		Red or yellow berries	Summer	Brown Thrashers, Catbirds, Cedar Waxwings, Purple Finches, Robins
	Winterberry	Red berries	Late summer to midwinter	Bluebirds, Brown Thrashers, Cardinals, Cedar Waxwings

Region	Shrub	Fruit or Flower	Season	Birds Most Often Attracted
South and Southeast Alabama Arkansas Florida Georgia Louisiana Mississippi North Carolina South Carolina Tennessee	American Elder	Blue-black berries	Late summer to midfall	Brown Thrashers, Cardinals, Carolina Chickadees, Chats, Flickers, Indigo Buntings, Mockingbirds, Phoebes
	Arrowwood	Blue-black berries	Fall	Brown Thrashers, Catbirds, Phoebes, Robins, White-eyed Vireos
	Bayberry	Gray berries	Fall to early spring	Downy Woodpeckers, Hermit Thrushes, Myrtle Warblers, Tree Swallows
	Black Haw	Blue-black berries	Fall	Carolina Chickadees, Downy and Red-bellied Woodpeckers, Hermit Thrushes, Mockingbirds
	High-bush Blueberry	Blue-black berries	Midsummer to midfall	Catbirds, Chats, Orioles, Phoebes, Tanagers
	Hybrid Weigela	Pink, red or white flowers	Spring	Ruby-throated Hummingbirds
	Many-flowered Cotoneaster	Red berries	Fall	Bluebirds, Cedar Waxwings, Mockingbirds, Robins
	Sapphireberry	Blue berries	Fall	Bluebirds, Cardinals, Catbirds, Mockingbirds, Summer Tanagers
	Siberian Dogwood	Blue-white berries	Fall	Bluebirds, Catbirds, Cedar Waxwings, Mockingbirds, Wood Thrushes
	Smooth Sumac	Red berries	Fall to early spring	Bluebirds, Carolina Chickadees, Catbirds, Downy Woodpeckers, Mockingbirds
North and South Central Kansas Manitoba Nebraska North Dakota Oklahoma South Dakota Texas	Beauty Bush	Pink flowers	Early summer	Ruby-throated and Rufous Hummingbirds
	Coralberry	Purple-red berries	Fall to midwinter	Hermit Thrushes, Purple Finches, Robins, Waxwings, Woodpeckers
	Fragrant Sumac	Dark red berries	Summer	Bluebirds, Red-headed Woodpeckers, Robins, Thrashers, Yellow-shafted Flickers
	Nannyberry	Black berries	Fall	Cardinals, Catbirds, Cedar Waxwings, Flickers, Hermit Thrushes, Robins
	Orange-eyed Butterfly Bush	Blue, pink, purple or white flowers	Midsummer to frost	Ruby-throated Hummingbirds
	Siberian Dogwood	Blue-white berries	Fall	Bluebirds, Cardinals, Chats, Evening Grosbeaks, Thrushes, Tree Swallows, Waxwings
	Siberian Pea Tree	Yellow flowers	Spring	Ruby-throated and Rufous Hummingbirds
	Winterberry	Red berries	Late summer to midwinter	Bluebirds, Brown Thrashers, Cardinals, Cedar Waxwings, Purple Finches, Robins

Region	Shrub	Fruit or Flower	Season	Birds Most Often Attracted
West and Southwest	American Elder	Blue-black berries	Late summer to midfall	Lewis' Woodpeckers, Magpies, Mountain Bluebirds, Sparrows, Thrushes, Warbling Vireos
Alberta Arizona Colorado	Black Haw	Blue-black berries	Fall	Hermit Thrushes, Robins, Townsend's Solitaires, Veeries, Waxwings
Idaho Montana Nevada	Nannyberry	Black berries	Fall	Bluebirds, Bohemian and Cedar Waxwings, Catbirds, Flickers, Hermit Thrushes
New Mexico Saskatchewan	Red Osier Dogwood	White berries	Summer	Bullock's Orioles, Cardinals, Hermit Thrushes, Mockingbirds, Swainson's Thrushes
Utah Wyoming	Running Serviceberry	Purple-black berries	Summer	Green-tailed Towhees, Lewis' Woodpeckers, Magpies, Swainson's Thrushes, Townsend's Solitaires
	Siberian Pea Tree	Yellow flowers	Spring	Broad-tailed Hummingbirds
	Snowberry	White berries	Midsummer to midwinter	Evening and Pine Grosbeaks, Magpies, Robins, Rufous-sided Towhees
	Staghorn Sumac	Red berries	Fall to early spring	Evening Grosbeaks, Hermit Thrushes, Magpies, Robins, Townsend's Solitaires
	Tatarian Honeysuckle	Pink or red flowers	Late spring	Broad-tailed Hummingbirds
		Red or yellow berries	Summer	Bohemian and Cedar Waxwings, Hermit and Swainson's Thrushes
Far West	Beauty Bush	Pink flowers	Early summer	Anna's, Black-chinned, Calliope, and Rufous Hummingbirds
British Columbia California	Blue Elder	Blue-black berries	Late summer	Black-headed Grosbeaks, California Thrashers, Phainopeplas, Steller's Jays, Swainson's Thrushes
Oregon Washington	Japanese Rose	Orange-red fruit	Fall	Evening Grosbeaks, Robins, Thrushes, Towhees, Townsend's Solitaires
	Magellan Fuchsia	Red and violet flowers	Early summer to frost	Anna's, Black-chinned, Calliope, and Rufous Hummingbirds
	Snowberry	White berries	Midsummer to midwinter	Black-headed, Evening, and Pine Grosbeaks, Robins, Spotted Towhees, Varied Thrushes, Wrentits

Reprinted from *The Time-Life Encyclopedia of Gardening/FLOWERING SHRUBS*, by James Underwood Crockett and the Editors of Time-Life Books. ©1972 Time-Life Books Inc., Publisher.

feed the fire, your winter birds will dig into the pupae and hibernating adult insects tucked away beneath the bark. One winter a Red-breasted Nuthatch daily worked over our woodpile.

Water

You and your backyard birds may be fortunate enough to have a pond or stream coursing through the backyard. Most of us will have to provide water for the birds to bathe in and drink. Birdbaths in whatever form they take will do the job. Make sure to keep them full during the summer, especially in hot, dry parts of the country such as the Southwest.

Birdhouses

Forty-eight species of birds have been known to nest in bird-houses or bird boxes, so you might want to give it a try in your back-yard. Decide what bird you'd like to get into a nesting box and find out its size requirements. Each species requires a specific size box with a specific size entrance. There is no guarantee you're going to get the bird you're after but there's a good chance a bird will nest in it. Bluebirds, titmouses, chickadees, wrens, Tree Swallows, and all woodpeckers nest in the hollows of trees and are likely candidates for a bird box. Robins, Barn Swallows, phoebes, Song Sparrows, and House Finches can all be attracted to nest on shelves. Shelves are attached to the side of a building, like your house or garage. The shelf can have all sides open or three, two, or one side open; it should have a slanted roof to keep the rain out. If you attach the shelf under the eave of your house you can dispense with the roof. Robins, Barn Swallows, and phoebes nest under eaves.

Purple Martin houses are another possibility, but unfortunately not for everyone. If you have an open lawn or meadow with a clear field of view, and I mean a clear field of view—no trees or manmade obstructions for at least forty feet in all directions—and you've heard rumors of Purple Martins in the neighborhood, then you have every reason to erect a Purple Martin house. It is mounted on a collapsible

Bird Box Dimensions

Kind of Bird	Size of Floor (in.)	Depth of Box (in.)	Height of Entrance Hole Above Floor (in.)	Diameter of Entrance Hole (in.)	Height to Fasten Above Ground (ft.)
Bluebird	5 × 5	8	6	1½	5–10
Chickadee	4 × 4	8–10	6–8	1⅛	6–15
Titmouse	4 × 4	8–10	6–8	1¼	6–15
Nuthatch	4 × 4	8–10	6–8	1¼	12–20
House Wren and Bewick's Wren	4 × 4	6–8	4–6	1–1¼	6–10
Carolina Wren	4 × 4	6–8	4–6	1½	6–10
Violet-green Swallow and Tree Swallow	5 × 5	6	1–5	1½	10–15
House Finch	6 × 6	6	4	2	8–12
Starling	6 × 6	16–18	14–16	2	10–25
Crested Flycatcher	6 × 6	8–10	6–8	2	8–20
Flicker	7 × 7	16–18	14–16	2½	6–20
Golden-fronted Woodpecker and Red-headed Woodpecker	6 × 6	12–15	9–12	2	12–20
Downy Woodpecker	4 × 4	8–10	6–8	1¼	6–20
Hairy Woodpecker	6 × 6	12–15	9–12	1½	12–20
Screech Owl	8 × 8	12–15	9–12	3	10–30
Saw-whet Owl	6 × 6	10–12	8–10	2½	12–20
Barn Owl	10 × 18	15–18	4	6	12–18
American Kestrel	8 × 8	12–15	9–12	3	10–30
Wood Duck	10 × 18	10–24	12–16	4	10–20
Prothonotary	5 × 5	8	6	1½	5–10

pole and has individual compartments, housing up to twenty-four Purple Martins. If the house is occupied with Purple Martins, your mosquito population will drop while the air above is filled with gurgling song and graceful flight. Enjoy.

One bird box sized for a particular species in a backyard of less than one acre is a rule that often doesn't apply. Any species that is the same size or smaller can move into that one bird box. Putting up several would increase your chances of getting the bird you're after. Also, Tree Swallow boxes can be as close together as thirty feet and are placed on posts in the open, near or standing in water. House Wrens need three or four boxes to consider before they select one. Place birdhouses on a pole stuck in the ground or on the side of a tree or building. You can build them or buy them. Bird-feeding catalogues usually feature them, including Purple Martin houses with collapsible poles. Following are the house dimensions for a number of popular bird box and shelf nesters.

Nesting Shelf Dimensions

Kind of Bird	Size of Floor (in.)	Depth Inside (in.)	Height to Fasten Above Ground (ft.)
Robin	6 × 8	8	6–15
Barn Swallow	6 × 6	6	8–12
Song Sparrow	6 × 6	6	1–3
Phoebe	6 × 6	6	8–12

Reprinted by permission of Alfred A. Knopf, Inc., from *The Audubon Society Encyclopedia of North American Birds*, by John K. Terres. Copyright © 1980 by John K. Terres.

USEFUL ADDRESSES AND PHONE NUMBERS

Dial-a-Bird

DIAL-A-BIRD services, also called Rare Bird Alerts or Hot Lines, give a prerecorded message listing birds of note recently sighted in your area, usually on a weekly basis. The report, prepared by one of your local bird clubs or Audubon groups, covers a lot more ground than your backyard, but it's a good way to compare notes, letting you know what's around and what rare species have been seen. If you don't find a phone number for your area in the following list, contact your local Audubon group or bird club for it.

Alaska
Anchorage Audubon Society 907-694-3504

British Columbia
Victoria Natural History Society 604-478-8534

California
Los Angeles Audubon Society 213-874-1318
San Francisco (Golden Gate Audubon Society) 415-843-2211
Santa Barbara Audubon Society 805-964-8240

Connecticut
Connecticut Audubon Council/Denison Pequotsepos Nature Center
  203-572-0012

Illinois
Central (Illinois State Museum) 217-785-1083
Chicago Audubon Society 312-675-8466

Maine
Portland, Maine, Audubon Society 207-781-2332

Maryland/Washington, D.C.
Audubon Naturalist Society of the Central Atlantic States
  301-652-1088

Massachusetts
Boston, Massachusetts, Audubon Society 617-259-8805

Michigan
Detroit Audubon Society 313-729-7140

Minnesota
Audubon chapter of Minneapolis/Minnesota Ornithologists' Union
  612-544-8315

New Hampshire
New Hampshire Audubon Society 603-224-9900

New Jersey
New Jersey Audubon Society 201-766-2661

New York
Albany/Hudson-Mohawk Bird Club 518-377-9600
Buffalo Museum of Science 716-896-1271
New York/Linnaean Society of New York/National Audubon Society
    212-832-6523

Ohio
Cleveland/Kirtland Bird Club 216-216-8186
Columbus Audubon Society 614-221-9736
Toledo Naturalists' Association/Maumee Valley Audubon Society
    419-531-4420
Walden Pond–Columbus Metropolitan Park Board 614-882-8325

Oregon
Portland Audubon Society 503-292-0061

Pennsylvania
Pittsburgh/Audubon Society of Western Pennsylvania 412-963-6104

Vermont
Vermont Institute of Natural Science 802-457-2779

Washington
Seattle Audubon Society 206-455-9722

Wisconsin
Milwaukee/Wisconsin Society for Ornithology 414-352-3857

Serious Study

Seminars in Ornithology: A Home Study Course on Bird Biology, Laboratory of Ornithology, Cornell University, 159 Sapsucker Woods Road, Ithaca, NY 14850.

For those of you who really wish to know your birds—inside and out—at the college level, noncredit, and at home, at your own time and pace. The course consists of nine seminars, each written by a leading ornithologist and edited by Olin Sewall Pettingill, Jr. It covers external and internal anatomy, migration, behavior, bird ecology, distribution, development, etc. You need no prerequisites, just your interest in birds. At the end of each seminar there are question sheets to be answered that are sent back to Cornell to be corrected and then sent back to you with the next seminar.

Bird Clubs

If you want to join a local bird club and share the experience, there's a good chance there will be one close by. The Audubon Society has 450 chapters throughout the country. To find an Audubon group close to your home, consult your telephone directory or write the society's national office in New York: National Audubon Society, 950 Third Ave, New York, NY 10022. Besides Audubon Society groups there are other local bird clubs you might locate by inquiring at your regional natural history museum, park, or forest district.

Breeding Bird Program

North American Nest Record Card Program, Laboratory of Ornithology, Cornell University, 159 Sapsucker Woods Road, Ithaca, NY 14850.

Here is an opportunity for you to become part of a nesting study that has been under way since 1965 and takes place anywhere you find a nesting bird, including your own backyard. The Laboratory of Ornithology and the National Audubon Society collect, process, and store data on the nesting biology of birds. Careful notetaking is expected, and amateurs or professionals can participate. You will receive printed cards to fill out as you observe the birds at the nest. The card has designated spaces for habitat description, nest description, dates, eggs, young, comments, etc. Once the cards are filled they are returned to Cornell or one of more than 150 regional centers. All contributors receive an annual newsletter, and any interested researcher, professional or amateur, can request the data to study.

Catalogues

Audubon Workshop, Inc., 1501 Paddock Drive, Northbrook, IL 60062. Squirrelproof and numerous bird feeders, houses, grain, baths, water heaters.

The Crow's Nest Bookshop, Laboratory of Ornithology, 159 Sapsucker Woods Rd., Ithaca, NY 14850. Feeders, houses.

Droll Yankee, Inc., Foster, RI 02825. Feeders.

Duncraft, 33 Fisherville Rd., Penacook, NH 03303. Feeders, houses, grain, baths.

Hummingbird Haven, 1255 Carmel Drive, Simi Valley, CA 93065. Hummingbird and oriole feeders.

Hyde Bird Feeder Co., 56 Felton St., P.O. Box 168, Waltham, MA 02254. Feeders, houses, grain, water heaters.

National Audubon Society Wild Bird Food, Box 207, Bristol, IL 60512. Grain.

Tri Manufacturing Co., Griggsville, IL 62340. Aluminum martin houses and mounting poles.

BIBLIOGRAPHY

IF YOU want to know more about a bird than its field marks you'll need more than your trusty field guide. There are numerous reference and how-to books on the market, so I'm going to make it easy for you. I am recommending four books that I call the essentials. If you are now beginning to build a library of bird books, begin with them. If for some reason they turn out to be your only purchases besides your field guide, you'll be well taken care of for years to come.

The Four Essentials

Bent, Arthur C. *Life Histories of North American Birds*. New York: Dover, 1919–68. An unabridged republication of the original United States National Museum edition. 23 volumes. Paperback.

Arthur C. Bent, under the auspices of the Smithsonian Institution, spent almost fifty years filling twenty-three volumes with a multitude of carefully selected details and observations, thoroughly covering each species of bird, describing its nesting, young, eggs, food, habits, behavior, habitat, distribution, and listing spring and fall arrival dates. What makes the text fascinating, giving the reader a sense of ornithological history, discovery, and immediacy, are the personal ob-

servations, not only from Bent himself, but from the journals of his contemporaries and from earlier naturalists like Audubon and Brewster. A bird's life history is drawn from all these different voices, from observations and notes taken from all over the country, covering a time span of sixty-five years, from 1875 to 1940. I derive satisfaction and reassurance from the consistency of nature when I compare my most recent observation with ones from Bent and find, lo and behold, they are the same. Most of the time they will be the same; a few discrepancies have, however, been found in Bent. This series is not the last word in a bird's life history, but it is one of the first. It is an important reference and starting point from which a birder can get to know a species and then begin to build its life history from his own observations. Don't feel compelled to buy all twenty-three volumes at once. Start with a family of birds or species you happen to be interested in.

Hickly, Joseph J. *A Guide to Birdwatching*. New York: Dover, 1975. 252 pages. Paperback.

This is a classic how-to of birding, covering the beginning phases of field identification and listing on to the more advanced phases of field work and ornithological endeavors. Even though this book was originally published in 1943, there hasn't been another book published since that inspires and informs the amateur, that broadens a student birder's approach to ornithology and the avifauna as does this forty-four-year-old book. Why it still holds up today has a lot to do with its author, Joseph J. Hickly, once professor at the University of Wisconsin and honored ornithologist. Hickly writes about the possibilities and the opportunities in ornithology available to the amateur and professional alike. He excites a reader's imagination, not only with his enthusiasm and knowledge of the subject, which are vast, but with the proposal of a question, with the presentation of simple data. Several of the subjects he covers are bird song, how to take notes and keep records, migration studies, bird counting, bird distribution, and bird banding. Hickly shows us what can be learned from simply sitting and observing, and he tells us what, where, and how to observe. By giving examples of various studies he provides the birder with possible studies to pursue himself. He includes an outline for a life history study, which, if followed, could keep a birder busy in his backyard for years to come. He cites such a birder, a woman who while raising five children spent eight years compiling a life history of the Song Sparrow from her backyard in Columbus, Ohio; today her work is considered an indispensable reference. Hickly provides us birders with options. He shows how we can pursue a study of the avifauna on our own time, enjoy the pursuit, and contribute to the collective study of ornithology—either from the field or the backyard. All that is required, he says, are the hours and careful notetaking.

Janovy, John, Jr. *Keith County Journal*. New York: St. Martin's Press, 1980. 210 pages. Paperback.

This book isn't, in the strict sense of the word, a reference. Nor is it a how-to book. So what is it doing here? Why do I so enthusiastically recommend it? My imagination is partially to blame; it has a life of its own. I envision you, the reader, reading these recommended volumes, and then I imagine your library of books growing—bird books, garden books, butterfly books, good books of all sorts—and I can't imagine your library without a copy of *Keith County Journal*. I can clearly see this book standing alongside all your other good books, tying all the diverse elements of nature together, like a unifying theory of matter that can be applied to your family, family car, backyard, and backyard birds. Meet John Janovy, professor of biology at the University of Nebraska. Janovy also happens to be an exceptional writer—a composite talent guided by the methodical and plotting mind of a scientist, the enthusiasm and curiosity of a student, and the vulnerability and concerns of a family man. He writes well because he is committed and involved with his job—the study and teaching of relationships. He writes about microscopic protozoa and their relationship to snails, termites, buffalo chips, swallows, wrens, rivers, students, teachers, and the flat endless plains of Nebraska. He writes about people and places, and they are always given names, first names if he writes about people. Read how a professor of biology, baffled by his empty Purple Martin house, thinks his way through to a solution and gets those birds to move in. Read how that same professor goes "Boy oh boy, oh boy" at the thought of listening to the tinkling sounds of pebbles as a Rock Wren leaves its nest. Several months after finishing *Keith County Journal*, I registered at a local college night school, taking Biology 101—in my middle forties and I was entertaining the thought of a bachelor's degree in biology! Obviously John Janovy's book unleashed something within. It is unlikely that you will enroll in Biology 101 as I did, but if you read this book you will have enjoyed a biology teacher and his students at work, and you will begin to understand and appreciate relationships between subtle and not-so-subtle organisms, including your relationship with your own backyard birds.

Terres, John. *The Audubon Society Encyclopedia of North American Birds*. New York: Knopf, 1980. 1108 pages. Hard cover.

Certain books look formidable even before they are opened; if they take you at all, they take you by surprise. Certain books when first picked up demand to be held securely, with a well-placed grip—you're immediately aware of their weight. As you thumb through the pages of such a book, scanning the text, looking over the illustrations, the heft of the book begins to take on the additional weight of excellence and accomplishment, and you find yourself turning the pages slowly and carefully, with anticipation. This is such a book—a monumental work, the result of a lifetime's study by the distinguished naturalist John Terres. The book includes 625 major articles on all aspects of bird life and biology; biographies of 847 birds; biographies of notable ornithologists; definitions of ornithological terms; 800 well-drawn black-and-white illustrations, diagrams, and maps. The comprehensive text and illustrations are alone worth the price, but the encyclopedia also features over 875 color photographs—probably some of the best color bird photography and reproduction to make it to a nine-by-eleven-inch printed page. They are a joy to look at.

Regional and Local References

If you'd like to know what birds to anticipate in your backyard then you should get yourself a regional guide for your area. They are inexpensive and come in the form of a slim paperback book that tells you what birds to expect in what habitat, when to expect them, and how abundant or rare they might be. Regional state guides can be found in Cornell's *The Crow's Nest Book Shop Gift Catalogue*: Write Laboratory of Ornithology, Cornell University, 159 Sapsucker Woods Road, Ithaca, NY 14850. Also, the American Birding Association carries most, if not all, of the state guides: Write American Birding Association, Inc., Box 4335, Austin, TX 78765. Ask for a birder's regional guide to your state and or area.

Attracting Birds

The following books will tell you how to prepare your backyard for the needs of your backyard birds. They contain plans and suggestions for building birdhouses, feeders, and baths and for establishing your own backyard wildlife sanctuary.

DeGraaf, Richard M., and Witman, Gretchin M. *Trees, Shrubs, and Vines for Attracting Birds*. Amherst: University of Massachusetts Press, 1981. 160 pages. Paperback.

Illustrated manual for creating bird habitats. One hundred sixty-two plants are covered, including their size and fruiting potential, range, fruiting period, propagation, and a list of birds that use the plant.

Harrison, George H. *The Backyard Bird Watcher*. New York: Simon and Schuster, 1979. 284 pages. Hard cover.

Harrison tells how to set up successful feeding stations, winter and summer, and how to select plants, choose bird seed, create a good water supply, care for injured birds, and solve pest problems. He provides model landscaping plans to attract birds, covering suburban and urban gardens.

Kress, Stephen W. *The Audubon Society Guide to Attracting Birds*. New York: Scribners, 1985. 337 pages. Hard cover.

"This book rests on the idea that bird populations will increase only when proper action is taken to remove limiting factors," writes the author. You remove limiting factors by improving and creating habitat. Kress tells you how to work with the landscape, improving and creating habitat, not only for a small suburban backyard, but for larger tracts of sixty to two hundred acres. His emphasis is land management, and that is where his book differs from some of the other books on attracting birds. He gives plans for gardens, pools, ponds, feeding stations, etc., and draws upon the experience of birders throughout the United States and Canada.

Martin, Alexander C.; Sim, Herbert S.; and Nelson, Arnold A. *American Wildlife and Plants: A Guide to Wildlife Food Habits*. New York: Dover, 1961. An unabridged republication of the 1951 McGraw-Hill edition. 500 pages. Paperback.

Guide to use of trees, shrubs, and grasses by birds and mammals. One thousand plant species covered. Three hundred North American birds are included with maps of their winter and summer ranges and graphs displaying the relative proportion of plant food consumed at each season.

Terres, John K. *Songbirds in Your Garden*. 3d ed. New York: Hawthorn Books, 1980. 228 pages. Paperback.

John Terres took time out from his lifetime work, *The Audubon Encyclopedia of North American Birds*, to write this basic bird-attracting reference. Not bad, for a breather. John tells you how to build birdhouses, feeders, and baths. He tells you what shrubs and flowers to plant to attract birds, covering different climatic conditions throughout the country. He includes a planning design for planting a backyard wildlife sanctuary, descriptions of flowering and fruiting seasons, and food preferences and nesting data for more of your common garden birds.

Periodicals

American Birds. Published six times a year by the National Audubon Society.

This magazine documents the changing bird life of the North American continent. Professionals and amateurs contribute material on bird behavior, feeding, nesting, identification problems, and population ecology. The magazine concentrates on reports of bird distribution in twenty-six reporting regions in the United States, Canada, the West Indies, and the Mexican border area. The January issue reports the findings of the winter bird population study and the breeding-bird census; March reports the fall migration; May, the winter season; July, the results of the annual Christmas Count; September, spring migration; November, the summer nesting season. Besides discovering what is going on in other parts of the country, you'll be able to see how your backyard birds compare to avian activity in your surrounding area. To subscribe write: *American Birds*, 950 Third Ave, New York, NY 10022.

Audubon. Published six times a year by the National Audubon Society.

Outstanding nature and wildlife photography. Equally outstanding coverage and writing dealing with the reason the magazine came into existence, birds, and also all aspects of the natural world, including diligent looks at the ups and downs of the environment. Les Line, *Audubon*'s editor, an excellent writer and nature photographer himself, is responsible for the magazine's high standards and the publishing of some of the best writers and photographers in the country. To subscribe write: National Audubon Society, Membership Data Center, P.O. Box 2667, Boulder, CO 80321.

Bird Watcher's Digest. Published six times a year by the Pardson Corporation.

Bird Watcher's Digest is printed on newsprint and only measures eight by five inches, but it covers the gamut of the birding experience: marathon birding, backyard birding, birders' big-year records, personal experiences and observations, and everything under the sun and moon. Roger Tory Peterson may author one article; Donald and Lilian Stokes, authorities on bird behavior, another; and you or your next-door neighbor another. Much of the material is selected reprints from newspaper articles about birds and birders. The magazine informs, gives the latest bird-watching gossip, and entertains. To subscribe write: *Bird Watcher's Digest*, P.O. Box 110, Marietta, OH 45750.

The Living Bird Quarterly. Published January, April, July, and October by the Laboratory of Ornithology at Cornell University.

If you become a member of the Laboratory of Ornithology at Cornell, you will not only help support the laboratory's research programs, but you'll receive *The Living Bird Quarterly*, a choice magazine covering the latest research, studies, and facts concerning all aspects of bird biology, written by working professionals and an occasional dedicated amateur. Look forward to excellent and numerous four-color bird photography. You will also receive their catalogue, *The Crow's Nest Book Shop Gift Catalogue*, from which you can buy, at membership discount, a large selection of bird books, field guides, regional guides, checklists, bird recordings, and various other bird-related items. This catalogue is an important resource and enjoyable to thumb through. For membership and subscription contact: Laboratory of Ornithology, Cornell University, 159 Sapsucker Woods Road, Ithaca, NY 14850.

Bird Songs

You may find the following recordings at some bookstores, in Cornell's *The Crow's Nest Book Shop Gift Catalogue*, advertised in *Audubon* or other birding magazines, or carried by local bird clubs or museums.

A Field Guide to Bird Songs (Eastern and Central North America). Boston: Houghton Mifflin. Two 12-inch, 33⅓ rpm records or three tape cassettes.
A Field Guide to Western Bird Songs. Boston: Houghton Mifflin. Three 12-inch, 33⅓ rpm records or four tape cassettes.

These two recordings, which correspond to Roger Tory Peterson's field guides, cover the songs of most of the North American species. Because of the numerous species represented, each species' song is short and does not cover regional dialects or other vocal variations; but don't let this deter you from selecting one or both recordings; with them you should have no problems learning to identify birds by their song.

Warblers. Sound and Nature Series. Donald J. Bower and William W. H. Gunn. Three 12-inch, 33⅓ rpm monaural records or two tape cassettes.

This is an excellent recording for those of us who need to learn and sort out all the subtle, varied vocalizations of the warblers. More than 325 examples of the calls and songs of all 57 North American species. Similar-sounding species are grouped together to permit comparison. Each species' song is well represented with vocal variations and regional dialects. This series also includes two other recordings: *Finches* and *Thrushes, Wrens, and Mockingbirds*.

Notes

Notes

Notes

Notes

Notes

Notes

Notes

Notes

Notes